ISBN-10:1500220035
ISBN-13:978-1500220037

i

HE FINALLY SURRENDERS

CORRESPONDENCE WITH MY FATHER

Mandy Margaret Bjordal

Daddy and his Girls

I have used fictitious names for my father's Australian ex-wife and son, his Norwegian wife and sons to protect their privacy.

DEDICATION

In loving memory of my beloved Father,

Harald Bjordal.

1915-1969

ACKNOWLEDGEMENTS

My sincere thanks go to the Embretsen family, in Norway, for finding me through my book "Where Do We Belong?' and for keeping in touch with me over two years.

Words are not enough to thank you, Kristoffer Holdmeide, for finding my Daddy's tomb at Our Saviour Cemetery at Var Frelser Gravlund, Norway.

Camilla Holdmeide, thank you for the information of this most esteemed and respected, large cemetery in Haugesund; established in 1911 and has World War II English soldiers buried there.

Thank you, son, Harald Matthew for the cover art portrait and Samuel Tang for the digital enhancement.

I am yet to personally meet Aud and Mette. God has blessed me to meet Hege and Nina daughters of my cousin Svanhild and her granddaughter Camilla and Paal Juelson who visited me here in Colorado.

Without Philo Ikonya, a journalist, who gave her views on Google about my first book *Where Do We Belong?* I would not have found my Norwegian family. God bless you Philo.

Prince David Kimera, my nephew in England thanks so much for finding a little about my Australian brother and my Daddy's trip to South Africa.

Last but not least, my heartfelt thanks go to Renêe Scott Tang for giving her time to edit and proof read my book and to organize the photographs settings.

INTRODUCTION
THE PREDICAMENTS

"Excuse me madame, the Headmaster wants a word with you at the office," said a smartly dressed secretary. In Africa you are never addressed by your first name but your marriage name or simply, *mama.* This was the second of December nineteen-sixty-nine: the last week of school term. I had started working at Westlands Primary School, Nairobi, that September after a three-month maternity leave. Several alternatives ran through my mind as to why Mr. Mackintosh wanted to see me; was I to be sacked for some unknown reasons? Did my husband or sister meet with an accident whilst going to work?

Only a week ago, on the twenty-seventh of November, my husband, baby and I had picked Sylvia at the Railway Station in Nairobi. She had spent half the holidays with Mummy in Kampala and the other half with Daddy up the mountain at Kigezi, Uganda. *Our parents separated when we were young.*

"Please, take a seat, Mrs. Louis," the Headmaster courteously pointed at a cushioned, wooden chair. Nervously seated I waited for the verdict.

"I have very disturbing news for you, Mrs. Louis." He said seriously. "Your husband…. Simultaneously my heart skipped a beat. I knew it. I knew it. Something terrible has happened to Romeo.

"Your husband and some Indian family from Parklands have called to say that your father died a week ago. I am so sorry. You have my permission to go home. Your husband will be here any moment to pick you," he sympathetically said, his blue eyes slightly misted.

"Died a week ago? My Daddy is dead? No, no. You must have been misinformed. My Daddy dropped Sylvia at the Railway Station on 26th November." I went on and on like a broken record with tears trickling down my face.

"How old was your father?" Mr. Mackintosh gently asked.

"He was old. Fifty-four," I said.

"That's not old. That's pretty young," he said. Looking at him I gathered he probably was the same age as my Daddy if not older. I was twenty four years old and Daddy was a good thirty years older than me.

Eh Daddy, how could you do this to me? I promised you I was coming next April, just five months away? I wanted you to meet my baby, Helen, and husband as well.

I went through disbelieve, doubt, anger. I stared at this English man wanting to tell him how strong my Daddy was- a Hercules. He did not sit behind a desk the whole day in a cool office but drilled rocks out in the steaming sun.

Daddy's death hit me like a hammer on the head. I couldn't think straight. It was like the slight stroke I had around my late forties. I was in a comatose state-like not knowing who I was. I've had a few of those in my life, each one different. Daddy is NOT dead. He was cautious about his health; eating right, not smoking or drinking and he walked up and down the mountain. When I started working at twenty he advised me to check my pressure. He blamed his health negligence causing his heart to enlarge.

"Mandy, I don't want you to land up like me when it's too late for doctors to do anything. Take care of your heart Mandy," Daddy advised me.

In 1968 I developed high blood pressure for no apparent reason. Dealing with doctors was certainly not my favourite piece of cake. I did, however, religiously take my children for checkups only then did I have my blood pressure checked. Actually Doctor Patel insisted I should.

Hardly had a half hour passed, in absolute solitude, at the school office stifling and reeking of floor polish, old books and furniture when Romeo and Sylvia arrived. Uncertain of how I would have handled the alarming news, Romeo collected the nurse first in case I needed first aid. I, on the other hand, expected delicate Sylvia to be completely distraught but she surprised me with her calmness. We endlessly cuddled without a sound or a tear.

Mummy always protected us from participating in Baganda funeral rituals. We did however attend Muslim after burial ceremonies. The Catholic faith had become an intrinsic part of my life. I buried several old nuns over the nine years I spent at the convent. I was unafraid to view colourless wrinkled–up bodies in an open coffin at Requiem Masses. Wanting special blessings, I kissed those icy-cold, angelic-looking faces. Practically brought up in a Convent School, death was something special: a joyous time when one finally goes to heaven. Catholics went to Heaven. Muslims to Jannah. I wasn't sure if it was the same place really.

Who was this man, Harald Bjordal, who had such an impact my entire life? He was *my* Daddy, the healthiest man on Planet Earth, a third child of a Norwegian family - the Bjordals, born 4th July 1915. Daddy spoke with warmth and eloquence about his two brothers and two sisters. He was proud of his mother, Britta Marie Jensdster and his Father, a merchant, who owned his own business.

When we visited Daddy in 1963 he interestingly watched us make the sign of the cross and praying before and after meals. Smiling, he commented, *"Talk about religion. You should meet my father, Jakob. No Lutheran is as committed as my father is. When we were little, we did nothing on Sundays but pray and literally fasted. When my mother was very ill with tuberculosis; my father singlehandedly took complete care of us."*

Grandpa, Jakob Bjordal, set such an impact on what a father should be that my Daddy followed his father's footstep. He talked to me privately about the *vicissitude* of rushed marriages. That marriage should be *reciprocal,* between two persons.

Things went sour for me, at barely five years old, when my pregnant Mummy left Daddy. To worsen matters, Daddy haphazardly rushed into a marriage to an Australian woman he briefly met in Mombasa on a three weeks holiday in January of 1950. Their church wedding lasted only three weeks! He called it *a shot-gun marriage.* If two marriages weren't enough, Daddy shortly visited his family in Norway 1951 and returned with a yet another young woman. Daddy never disclosed his complicated life to any of us until 1967 when he confided in me.

Whilst in college 1966, Daddy informed me about his enlarged heart caused by an abnormal heartbeat, arrhythmia. Having no knowledge what he was talking about I ran to Sylvia, my closest sibling, a nurse. She said arrhythmia, high blood pressure and rheumatic fever can cause the heart to enlarge. We were about to lose a father we deeply loved. When? We could not foretell.

As far I was concerned people died at an ancient age. At least that is what I saw with Mummy's extended family. I therefore went through denial for two years: the thought eating me like a cancer. I could not accept it. My strong Daddy isn't going to die. Between the years of 1967 to 1969 Daddy tried hard to prepare me for his coming death using riddles.

"Mandy, I want you to save a little of your earnings for a rainy day. I may leave this wretched world and I do not want you to suffer or be harmed. Build your life and help your sisters when you can." I naively thought he meant leaving *wretched* Uganda which was becoming politically unstable by the day. I asked him whether he was planning to retire in Norway. *No,* he assured me, *I will never leave you.* His letters were evidence of his coming death rather than just a fatherly duty toward a daughter. Rather than see me worried he covered up the seriousness of his heart condition with excuses of; *wretched flus, bloody allergies, virus and parasites. "That is the damned reason I don't feel too well."* Soon Daddy's cheerful character changed to unhappiness. In 1963, I wished I were at the mine taking care of him now that, his wife, Ulfhild left him taking her two sons along. In one of his latest letter to me his wife signed; *Harald is sick and I don't know where money will come from to take care of the family.*

When Ulfhild and their sons left, Uganda was still a paradise. My uncle King Mutesa II was in power helped by Prime Minister Milton Obote. It was not until 1972 that Uganda substantially worsens. Idi Amin expelled millions of Indians; the biggest exodus East Africa ever experienced. Europeans, the English or Arabs were not targeted. After Daddy's funeral that was the end of my visits to my beloved hometown. Not till 1989, twenty years later, when my dear Grandma died.

Although the convent schools had toughened me up, I was unprepared to face the world without Daddy; my guardian angel. No more monthly letters to pick me up when I stumbled. Letters that wiped out nuns' negative warning of, *"Wait till you go out into the world and find out what life is all about."* Letters that did not speak of treacherousness, deceitfulness, and uncouth characters lurking all over the city. Negativities never existed in my life when Daddy was alive.

Seeing us growing up, in leaps and bounds, Daddy worriedly advised me not to marry until I was at least twenty five years old and not to get *in a family way,* until we had *'learnedt'* the man. When I had a baby he said, *"Do not to leave baby with a nanny to nurture her when you should."* Taking my late Daddy's advice, over the years, I carried my babies in wicker baskets to work with permission granted from the English Headmaster. I probably was the first teacher daring enough to do that.

"'Grandpa is dead. I wanted him to lovingly hold you," I tearfully told my smiling toothless six month old baby.

A couple of weeks ago before his death, Daddy had scrutinized baby Helen's photograph I had sent him and was anxious to meet *Helene*, as he called her. Daddy missed me very much that November. With those weird feelings of mine I had told Romeo we should visit Daddy that August but he planned it for April 1970. I never forgave myself for not following my instinct.

I was enthralled hearing the wonderful, peaceful holiday Sylvia bubbled about. Together they enjoyed rowing a boat in the very blue Kazinga Lake I had been at, surrounded by high mountains as far as the eyes could see. They watched fluorescing colours in the sky thinning ominously before going home. The world belonged to them. With Daddy we owned the world. I looked at the photograph of my shirtless, smiling, healthy-looking Daddy, noting the soft, blonde hairs on his freckled arms that I had stroked as a child: his generous smile conveying extraordinary joy. I then scrutinized another photo Sylvia took two weeks before they left for Kampala.

"Daddy doesn't look well in this photo. He looks tired. He has put on slight weight around his tummy," I concernedly said to Sylvia. Daddy could no longer weather his hard and drudging existence anymore.

"I promise you, Margaret. Daddy is fine," Sylvia assured me.

"Oh yes, I almost forgot. Here is a letter Daddy wrote on twentieth of November at Hunts, his English lawyer's, office. Daddy asked me to personally deliver it to you when he dropped me at the Kampala Railway Station," Sylvia happily said.

"Daddy actually dropped you at the Railway Station? Lucky devil," I said enviously. That was something I had always longed for when little. My ever tearful, beautiful Mummy saw us off for years. I will never forget the segregation that existed in those days; each colour at the designated compartments. Craning my neck, like a flamingo, at clustered train windows along narrow corridors, I searched for Daddy. He might just turn up: I had hoped.

Every holiday Daddy showed us photos of our growing up brothers. *"Both the boys are a head taller than me. Haakon has grown his hair like the Beatles and if I'm not mistaken he has started smoking."* My Norwegian brothers Haakon and Braaken went to an

English boarding school in Kenya (Nakuru or Naivasha) when very young. Daddy said, " *The bloody English Headmaster picked on Braaken. It's unfortunate the English kept a grudge against the Norwegians because of King Harald Hardrada, the last Viking King. He terrorized and hacked the English to death and temporarily ruled England before he was killed on the battlefield. Don't ever think that Africans are the only people mistreated by white people. When Norwegians escapees landed in Demark for safety they were made slaves during World Wars,"* Daddy explained. He then smiled and said since Norway was ruled by many Haralds. *"You never know I could be a prince."* On reading Bryce Courtenay's book, *The Power Of One,* later on in life I learnt how Afrikaans boys mistreated English boys and realized what Daddy had said was true.

Next morning 28th November 1969, at around seven, I woke up with severe palpitations and was sweating. Romeo asked me what the matter was.

"I've had a terrible dream. Daddy was driving back to Kabale when suddenly he felt a terrible chest pain. He stopped at the side road of Masaka, put a booklet across his chest and raised his hands up and died."

The dream was four hours before Daddy, assumingly, died that very day at eleven in the morning. Had Africa been as modernized as it is today, with cell phones and modern communication devices, I would have warned him not to travel but rather get admitted at Mulago Hospital. I once told Daddy some of my frightening dreams had actually materialized. Daddy smiled and said I was telepathic. At least he never made fun of me as friends and family did.

Before leaving Africa I once dreamt of a Mkamba neighbour's nephew committing suicide. This young man was at a lovely lone field with a rope. Throwing it up over a steady branch, he secured it, wound it around his neck and hung himself. I wanted to warn the family but Romeo was against it. *"You and your dreams, Meggie. Don't go frightening people."*

A week or two later I met the lady at South B shopping centre. We casually talked. I had forgotten all about my dream. I asked her why she did not come to our yearly New Year's barbecue. She said her young nephew hung himself on a lone field in Machakos on such and such date that December! I did not tell her I had dreamt it.

Here in Colorado, one morning I awaken from a disturbing dream about my Scottish-Kikuyu friend, Gillian, being shot. A man came to her clinic, shot her as she threw something at him. She held her chest asking the nurses to call her Mother and collapsed. Blood flowed around her like a little red pool.

Sometime after arriving at Colorado, USA, 2002 Elvira, a friend of mine, called me from France. First question I asked was about Gillian.

"Didn't you know? She was killed three weeks ago." And I was given details exactly as I had dreamt. As she threw the key of the safe to the thug, as he had demanded, he shot her! The killer was never found.

Before leaving Kenya I had invited Gillian to collect flower plants for her hospital at semi-arid Athi Rivers. As the gardener got busy with selecting, digging and loading plants into an empty lorry we sat and had tea. Gillian encountered two episodes held at gun point on Mombasa Road. I outpoured my recent execution experience.

One day a mother brought two little children for tutoring. Out of nowhere two men appeared and demanded the car keys. Watching what was taking place from the kitchen window, I realized there was trouble. Walking to the gate something diverted me to open one of the dogs' cages. I then slightly opened the main gate; hoping the two children would come to me. But they were in a hysterical state of mind and would not budge; crying, tightly holding on their mother's legs; a gun at her head.

I truly believe God directed me to leave one of the dogs' doors ajar. In Africa we have kennels on the outside next to the car park. One of the men rushed at me pointing a gun at my head and ordered me to go indoors. Both dogs viciously bared their teeth at the man. I asked Jesus why was He letting me die this way; when I was about to immigrate to America? A sudden calmness came over me.

In times of danger, one is filled with heroism. My plan was to switch on the alarm at the kitchen door. That would have caused a bullet in my head. Miraculously, when I turned around not a soul was there. The dogs baring their teeth made the thieves run for their lives; shooting in the air like American highway men in movies. They stole another car and drove away only to stall on the highway because of no petrol (gas). I went through shock and a feeling of emptiness just as I felt when Daddy died. We have no grief therapy as such in Africa, only family and friends' support. A very committed Catholic neighbour came over to console and pray over me.

Gillian, advised me to go to America even though it was much against my love for Africa; very much like Daddy. He immensely loved Africa and became a

xiv

Ugandan Citizen two years before his death.

There was this unexplainable void within me the moment Sylvia arrived on November twenty-seventh up to second of December nineteen-sixty-nine.

In the letter Sylvia brought me, Daddy had written his disappointment of his wife leaving him. It was not a legalized divorce but a self-imposed separation. He confided in me that he was planning to see the lawyer and change his will leaving everything to his children. Reading his last letter I immediately wrote warning everyone not to burden Daddy with complains. He was a sick man. I had hoped Ulfhild would stay on with Daddy when Sylvia and I met her in 1967. She and the boys visited in 1968 for the last time.   When   I learnt that Ulfhild was back in Uganda April of 1970 to sort out Daddy's business; the first thing I asked her was to kindly send me back my last letter to Daddy. She wrote back that Mr. Demitrius had misplaced it.

"Anyway, I don't think there was anything of importance." How heartless was that at this most hurtful phase of my life when the sore was still raw? Could I as a mother be this mean to my stepchild? I honestly do not remember what I had written, except; *I love you Daddy."*

"Do not worry Mandy. Demitrius cannot read English," I heard Daddy say and was comforted.

As I sat with Daddy one evening, at his office, he showed me a hidden file with my letters methodically stored under lock and key since 1956. My Daddy knew how I hated my letters being read by someone else. I was touched to the very depth of my heart.

Nothing resembling privacy ever existed in my life; the nuns, mischievous friends, even Mummy could get someone to read them for her. I too kept Daddy's letters under lock and key in a small brown suitcase.

Being my usual suspicious self I asked Daddy if I could have my letters back.

"Certainly not. They are mine," Daddy said teasingly. *"I re-read them and have realized you could become a writer."*
"You think so Daddy? My English is terrible!" I said humbly. *"Well, read a lot and you will get there."* Even now at over twenty one he still encourages me.

Daddy and I corresponded twice a month that is approximately twenty four letters per year. Multiply that by ten or eleven years, one hundred and ninety two letters to be exact. I wondered if Ulfhild burnt *my* letters in the fireplace after Daddy died. I hope she did. What about the Australian ex-wife, Marjory's and son R. David's photographs Daddy had shown me? I see them now; two beautiful people I never met.

Daddy died with a presence of mind. He rolled up the car windows, placed his passport on his chest for identification, and locked up the car in case of thugs. How urgently he must worked those few vital moments? That was exactly as I had dreamt. The booklet that I saw was the passport the police found on his chest.

Before proceeding on long trips Daddy made sure to see his Norwegian doctor at Mulago Hospital for travel confirmation.

"Daddy, did you pray or curse?" I wondered. Annoyance easily triggered Daddy's temper at times.

I never realized Daddy knew much of the Bible, Church History and even the Koran much better than any of us. I once told Daddy I was praying for him to become a Catholic.

"Do you think I am an awful sinner if I am not Catholic? I do not smoke or drink, nor pick women in bars or streets. I help those in need never expecting to be paid back. I feed three hundred hungry workers. Christian organizations are ever on my case for donations. I've got to help them otherwise I'll never hear the end of it." I wished I hadn't suggested that. He knocked me hard on the head making me feel guilty.

Daddy taught me never to point an accusing finger at people who did not believe in what I believed. Nor make fun of people's languages, customs, or diet.

"If one slogs from morn to eve, as I do, and become as tired as a dog, is there time to sin? An idle mind is the devils' work tool. Remember that, Mandy. In any case where is temptation living here like a hermit?" He gently asked me. Of course, I knew that.

I had lived in *heaven* where I felt God's presence like no other place. No one talked about God when I was little. But I felt unexplainable beings protecting me.

The hustling and bustling, of Romeo, in the bathroom and my daughter, Jacqueline, next door woke me up feeling unusually cold though I was under a thick blanket. I was on mid-term weekend the year of 1996. Romeo normally did not wake me up. Try as I may I could not move nor open my eyes. I wondered if I was breathing at all but wasn't sure. Oh well, when Romeo kisses me goodbye he will find out I'm unconscious and call an ambulance. He had insured me with AAR (Kenya). I heard him leave. *Oh no! Romeo is leaving and so is Jacqueline.* She usually popped her head in our bedroom and said *I'm off mum.* Today she didn't.

Realizing I was left at God's mercy the first thought that came to mind was Daddy. I bet he too wished for someone to help him. *Am I dying Daddy?* Lucky me, I thought, God has given me time to pray the Act of Contrition. By end of the prayer, realizing I still was very much alive and clear of thought I prayed the Acts of Faith, Hope and Charity then a whole Rosary. No doubt I felt extremely cold and could not move or open my eyes. I then asked Jesus; *why don't You send Joseph over? Perhaps I'd gain consciousness if he shakes me.* No sooner had I requested that of Jesus when I heard a knock at the door. Joseph had worked for me over fifteen years.

"M*ama, Mama why aren't you up its ten O'clock."* He shouted behind the closed door.

Open the door Joseph, open the door. I tried answering but no voice came out. Joseph slowly opened the door, peered in, came over to my bed and shook me and I gained consciousness. I told him what had happened and he said he was worried and was about to call Bwana, but decided on checking me first. He said, "I knew something was wrong. You never wake up this late."

What would any sensible person have done but rush to the Catholic Hospital ten minutes away and had a thorough checkup? *I never did!* So I have a slight defect on the right ventricle.

"Why did you have your hands up, Daddy? Did you finally surrender? Were you making it easy to be identified? Most likely. How I wish I knew what went on in his mind at that moment.

Twelve years later, I sat with Daddy's beloved daughter Sylvia her cold hands in mine, her hazel wistful eyes staring past me as I helplessly looked at her ashen face. Like Daddy, she stretched forth her arms, as did my little friend in school before dying. *Do dying people do that?* I couldn't imagine Daddy, at sixty-five, accepting lively Sylvia's death. Would we have travelled together to England to see her? Most likely. But, God took Daddy twelve years earlier at a young age of fifty-four. I wonder if Daddy and Sylvia met in heaven? Maybe, maybe not. I believe seeing God is so overwhelming nothing distracts you not even family.

A Catholic priest, friend of Daddy, drove past and waved at him at around twelve O'clock. That's what they normally did. I wished he had stopped and blessed my Daddy.

In those days, people never ate whilst driving. Daddy normally stopped by the wayside for lunch and a drink. Many travellers waved at him capturing his warm smile as he waved back. But not that day. I wished Scotland Yard could solve this mystery for me.

Did he swallow the wrong medication by mistake; as I once did when a sciatica pain in my leg was killing me? I walked into a clinic downtown and met a South Indian doctor with an English name, V. Taylor. *He didn't look half white like me.* As always my curiosity got the better of me and I asked about his surname. He smiled and said when the British ruled India servants adapted their masters' surname. Those names were carried through generations.

Doctor Taylor prescribed strong sleeping tablets, specifically, to be taken at bedtime, some pain killers and a third I don't remember what for. After anxiously swallowing two tablets at the Chemist, I dragged my aching leg towards the Holy Family Cathedral for mass. The pain increased by the minute and I blew air out like a woman in labour becoming parched. Passing my legless beggar friend enjoying a kindly given 'fish and chips' meal; he invited me to join him. I thanked him saying I'd be late for mass. I stopped at an Indian Bookshop and asked for water and a seat. I then attended mass but had to limp out of church due to the pain. I drove like a drunkard along Mombasa Road luckily there was no traffic. At the junction a policeman stopped me but on seeing the condition I was in, he let me go home. Getting out of the car, without pulling the handbrake, I collapsed on the couch, unconscious. Romeo and my son, Harald, came home at around five in the evening and gently woke me up. I shouted at them not to touch me. I then saw gold chains at my son's feet and asked him to pick them up. I was hallucinating.

Did you take the wrong amount of tablets as I did, Daddy? I wondered.

That evening the same priest was surprise to see Daddy still sitting in the car, with arms up, the cheeks sun-burnt. He tried opening the door but they were all locked. Off he rushed to the nearest police station and they came over, broke the door lock and took the remains to Mulago Mortuary.

Did you watch them do that, Daddy?

The police kindly broke the news to Mummy and took Brother Frank to identify the body. Somehow the family got in touch with Helene in Soroti. She had no idea how to get in touch with me but randomly rang an Indian family in Parklands, Kenya, begging them to find me at Highridge Primary School in Westlands.

"What killed you Daddy? Do people with enlarged

hearts die that way?" Daddy often got irregular and rapid heartbeats when we took evening walks up the mountains and he made me feel his pulse. I hated doing that but he smiled.

Rushing to the funeral Sylvia, Romeo, baby Helen and I almost died. Romeo drove like a maniac, late that evening, missing a detour sign. We went flying up in the air and landed with a thump onto a tarmac road below. We had no seat belts, baby Helen was in a wicker basket like baby Moses, yet we were intact; an absolute miracle.

"Did you save us, Daddy?"

I honestly did not see the need of rushing. For all I know Daddy might as well been buried by his Norwegian family. Daddy's elder brother Tormod had a stroke. On one holiday Daddy talked to me about being cremated. *"I'd love my ashes strewn on my mountain and garden."* I did not like that hurtful joke. I had never heard of anyone cremated except the Hindus.

A man dressed in a white overcoat wheeling Daddy's remains on a bed disrupted my thoughts. Not a word was uttered or sympathy given. And he left. *My* Daddy looked so young, fresh and peaceful as if in a deep sleep. Daddy was sunburnt. If only I could peel off that skin and smoothen his frozen face. But I could not budge. How bravely I had kissed dead nuns yet I could not kiss my own Daddy.

"What happened, Daddy?"

Sylvia, bravely uncovered Daddy's chest exposing a V cut haphazardly stitched. *"They shouldn't have done that to my Daddy!"* Complained my mind.

Sylvia and Helene, both nurses, assured me that is what is done to the dead. Sylvia further explained that white people normally turn blue when they die of heart problems. Daddy didn't. My supporter, Romeo, met the remains but not the real man I so often talked about. His Greek son-in-law, George, was there too.

Just as we got out of the room on top floor, a loud debated conversation at ground floor about Mr. Bjordal aroused our attention. As we peered downstairs, to our surprise, we encountered Mr. Demitrius, the manager, and an unknown European man. Looking down overpowering memories nearly toppled me over.

I had actually loved this short, jolly, very talkative friendly, *Mickey Rooney,* Cypriot manager. He once invited us to a spicy, tasty Greek dinner. Daddy's eyes pooled with tears and his face redden. Sitting at the coffee table Mr. Demitrius introduced us to his beautiful family, in a leather bounded album, a wife and two children in Cyprus: a country way behind in development.

After Daddy died the man didn't think we existed although he knew where we lived. I wondered how he got the news in Kabale. Perhaps, Mr. Hunts, the English lawyer, sent him a telegram. As said before, Ulfhild was in Norway since 1963 with a short visit in 1967 and 1968. That August Daddy fulfilled our wish of meeting our half-brothers for the first time. Unfortunately I was in Mombasa, with college mates, enjoying brilliant white sand beaches and taken to a real coral island in a glass-boat.

As we watched the ashes sparkle red; a thought sparked my mind. If only I could steal a little of the hot ashes from the pyre and fulfil Daddy's wish sprinkling his ashes on his mountain.

"Be careful Mandy. You do not want to burn your fingers," I heard him say. That's how he cautioned me up in *my heaven* when I wanted to fly on the clouds

beneath our feet; *gravity will inexorably pull you down, Mandy.*

As we stood in stillness watching the wind-skirling smoke across, my mind wandered.

"Was your body washed, Daddy? Were you dressed in the only black suit you had? Were you in a cushioned coffin or were you wrapped like an Egyptian mummy and lay on the pyre?

We alone, his four daughters, our two husbands, possibly brother Frank and the Norwegian Ambassador, fully dressed in a black suit and tie were present for the cremation. *"I was given two O'clock,"* he said checking his Rolex watch for assurance. We gave no respond. Watching too many James Bond movies I imagined conspiracy. I bet these ashes aren't Daddy's. His body must have been flown to Haugesund, Norway and given a decent funeral. *'Daddy, you weren't deceitful. Please help me solve this mystery.'*

Being suspicious, Sylvia and I had, earlier on met Daddy's Doctor at Mulago Hospital trying to find out if Daddy had gone for his checkups. *"Yes he did. Nothing life-threating, no chronic cough or wheezing was found. He was absolutely fine."* The doctor said tears filling up his dark blue eyes.

"Could for some reason the cremation time been changed?" I thought as I tearfully watched a disturbed cool wind blowing the pale-grey ashes in confusion. I wondered if the ashen skeletal body was truly *my* Daddy's. Did his gold-plated tooth melt at the pyre or was it extracted? I remembered a small tattoo on his arm.

"I did this when I was a sailor." Daddy told me pointing at his tattoo. What a wonderful trip that was on

xxiii

a Portuguese ship, the Santa Cruz de Tenerife. A young jolly twenty-three year Harald Bjordal travelled from Morocco, North Africa, down the Red Sea passed Tanzania and all the way to South Africa in nineteen thirty-eight.

This *SS Duncluce Castle* ship was built by Swans Company in Glasgow and Dumbarton, England a prominent British shipping line. It operated passenger fleets and cargo ships between Europe and mainly South Africa as early as nineteen hundred. This was before the Anglo-Americans landed in Morocco and Algiers in nineteen forty-one, four years before I was born. Charming Daddy played sing-along tunes on his accordion.

Year after year, I pent-up my grief as I buried ex-school mates and friends' parents in dignity at Langata Cemetery in Kenya. I was unable to do that for Daddy even if I wanted to. First born or not we had no power. Daddy belonged to another family across the sea.

Doctors had advised Daddy to retire but he never flaunted. *"How can I when my sons are still in school and Ulfhild is permanently ill?"* How unfair is it to die alone at the roadside with not a soul to help you; without dignity, like a criminal or an animal.

Although Mummy objected on Hindu cremations, she encouraged us to support our father. Persisted, pestering questions kept bothering me. My life has always been an unfathomable mystery.

One holiday Daddy caught me silently puzzling over the fingerless Cypriot manager. Reading my mind Daddy told us a funny story about Demitrius. Daddy was out of the country when this accident occurred.

"Mr. Demitrius never stops talking even when working. As he oiled a machine he distractedly gave orders when chop the machine took off his four fingers! He drove himself over three hundred miles to Mulago Hospital bleeding like hell and collapsed there."

I thought Daddy would have a huge funeral; manager Demitrius, the government groups that stopped over at Daddy's before proceeding to the Congo.

"Hundreds of Government people sleep over as if my home is a hotel. Not only that, landing on me unexpectedly and expecting me to bend backwards entertaining them when I am a very ill man, Mandy."

A proper funeral would at least been a vent for real grief instead of doubt profoundly effecting me my entire life. Looking through the obituary section in the Newspaper I searched for Daddy's death announcement. There was nothing. The lawyer or manager or even Ulfhild could have announced his death. Uganda Radio Station spends an hour every day announcing deaths. My Grandma said *her son Biodal* should be buried at the outer land around the Royal Tombs at Kasubi; if not at her burial land in Bombo. But we had no rights. Ulfhild had.

Not to worry Daddy we put you in the Kenya Nation Newspaper letting friends in Kenya know we had lost you.

How often did Daddy tell me, *"This is a wretched world, Mandy. You got to always be prepared."* This was not my jolly Daddy speaking. He always said how beautiful Africa was *not wretched.*

I am now sixty-eight, living in Colorado. When I feel hapless or when ill I re-read Daddy's well preserved letters for guidance. *"Hold your head up,*

Mandy. Be proud of who you are. You have very good genes, besides intelligence. Remember to check-up your blood pressure. With modernization your heart can be fixed."

Daddy dreamt of retiring in America. *"I'll get your freckles removed. I know they bother you so much, Mandy. That's what beautiful actress Shirley McClain did,"* he once said to me. He truly admired her. A good thing, my skin darkened and the freckles blended in. Daddy would have been amazed with what plastic surgeons do today. People get heart transplants, pig valve, pacemakers, and even bypass. The heart is controlled with digitalis and diuretic. My pulse has been slowed with Atenolol the past twenty years.

I remember in 1967, we visited a Greek miner, friend of Daddy for lunch. It was there, for the very first time, I saw a Greek child with heart problems. It frightened the daylight out of me. His hands and lips were blue. His father was determined to try South Africa's Doctor Bernard who successfully did the first heart transplant. Daddy said if this boy's operation succeeds he too would go for it. I still believed *my* Daddy was fine. He had no blue lips or hands. The only strange thing I noticed about Daddy was that he would suddenly go very red in the face then drowse off even whilst driving. Many times I'd gently tap him on the thighs and he'd say, *"You think I'm asleep Mandy?"*

Nineteen sixty-seven was a bad year for Daddy. The government imposed health insurance requirements for the over three hundred workers. My disheartened Daddy temporarily closed the mine. Even *we* his children had no a health insurance.

"Mandy dear, because no one reaches into his pocket and gives back the money I loan them my life is

a mess in this Godforsaken country. The government takes 75% of every twenty shilling I make." That year he had hoped to send me to England and Sylvia to France. I tearfully read the letter at Maryhill School where I worked as a teacher.

Just last holiday, in 1968, we went out to dinner at a Greek restaurant. The Juke-box's flashes of red and green lights caught my eyes. I walked over and saw a selection of Pat Boone, Ricky Nelson, Sammy Cooke, Nat King Cole and many more small records to choose from. I timidly asked Daddy for a shilling to play some of my favourites. He smiled and gave me a crispy ten shillings note. *Keep the change, Mandy.* As the music played, I thoughtfully watched my brilliant fifty-three year-old Daddy seriously discussing business with a friend. I kept alert in case Daddy threw a question at me; generally on politics or business. Luckily, he talked about how proud he was of: *my beautiful daughters.* Discrimination between daughters was at its peak in East African. Money was not worth wasting on daughters when they were to be another man's wife.

Rather than selfishly burying Daddy's wisdom and love with me when I die I've decided to share it. Hoping, mainly, that R. David Bjordal, will one day find this book about the father he never knew. Hopefully, my Norwegian brothers who saw him only thrice between the years of 1963 to his death 1969 will know the true man their father was. For our children and grandchildren. Last but not least for my second cousins; Nina, Mette, Aud, Hege and their children who never knew their Granduncle.

Daddy on the Santa Cruz 1938

Mine life with Daddy included hunting 1948

CHAPTER ONE
BACK THEN

Here I am, one happy-go-lucky little girl floating, in *heaven,* with my jovial Daddy.

Watching sky-activities is one of our favourite past-time. *Our heaven is way up, seven thousand feet above sea level.* A fury, infinite yellow-red bulb slowly descends behind blackened mountains. Both of us literally adore Sun's introspective and stunning wife, Moon. She always smiles down at us. Instantaneously *heaven* is filled with joyous trills of millions minute night creatures settling down to sleep. Angels' breaths elongate Moon's yellow reflection on the surface of our lake far beyond. *My* Daddy made that lake. Together with workers, slightly taller than me, they dug up clayey soil as high as a mountain making a huge, deep hole. *"NEVER play over there!"* Daddy warns me. Soon heaven will open up and mighty rains and torrents of water will rush down cliffs and fill up this dangerous hole. (Our long rains are due in March to May). *Our rain does not bruise nature.*

After the rains slacken, peace reigns. Daddy holds my little hand which disappears in his large, warm palm. Smiling down at me he says there's a wonderful surprise awaiting me. I skip happily alongside Daddy's long strides. As we walk he points to mountain peaks looming ahead of us touching another higher heaven. There we are at this lovely big lake covered with hundreds of water birds happily diving in and swimming. How I wish I were a bird or a duck. Daddy will soon culture fishes. We both love fish. As for water plants they'll gradually find their way around *our* lake

1

and beautify it. I am so proud of my Daddy. He can do anything. See; he made a home so quarrelsome birds could be happy. Whenever we appear, workers stop working and low incantations arise. Daddy greets them in Luchiga, *Osibireje*? How are you? *"Ni barunji, we are well,"* they answer.

After a day's hard work Daddy swims stark naked shocking invisible people peering behind bushes. He is careful not to do this in front of my Muslim Mummy or us.

"When I travelled down to Africa, most people were half-naked. Right up to Ethiopia, the Sudan and Kenya. Why should a naked white man shock them?" Daddy told me years later as I looked at photographs of various, naked, indigenous people in Africa.

Sitting out on the verandah above the lightly pink clouds, we inhale the cool, fresh air.

"That will expand your lungs, Mandy," he resolutely says in Kiswahili. When I grow up, I want to have strong lungs like Daddy. In the evening, as huge mercury light looks down on us, Daddy's slick, top hair turns silver. I too turn my back to the moon and ask Daddy if my hair becomes silver. Daddy agrees, tousling my ash-blonde hair. I likewise ruffle his thick darker-blonde hair cascading down his neck.

Pointing to the moon stationed at the high, serene blackened mountain peaks, the moss covered cliffs, and darkened emerald lake, Daddy tells me to store those magnificent scenes in my brain. When I grow up I will paint them. True to his words, rocks and scrubs across vast moon-washed spaces, forlorn shadow in moon-flooded nights are still etched back of my mind. Daddy is musically minded. When relaxed he plays the accordion and sings in the Norsk language, encouraging

2

me to sing along. I get the tune but never the words. Still, I love the sound of Daddy's deep voice and his crystal blue eyes liken rivers, or lakes or sky. Clouds literally pass through them. That immensely fascinates me.

Daddy further explains that the world is mighty huge. There are millions of people with every colour hair, skin, and eyes. I thought that my beige siblings, three hundred Africans, and four whites were the only existence in our solitary world. I was yet to meet Indians, Europeans and Arabs in Kampala.

Every other morning I watch Daddy brushing his chin with a soapy substance using a knife-like blade to remove the little sprouts of hairs! Then he pats a faint tinge of aftershave. That smells pleasant.

"*Mandy dear, never touch this. It will cut you,*" he intones the dire consequences in a level voice. Bending over, he let me feel the sharpness of the knife as well as the smoothness of his now paler chin and side-cheeks. Daddy dresses in khaki shorts, a short-sleeved shirt and long turned-down socks a little below the knee and safari boots from a Bata Shoe company in Kampala, which imported shoes from an English country, Kenya.

"*Kenya is as good as South Africa where I once worked at a mine.*" I am told.

Feeling bored with Mummy, as she is always busy with this new baby girl '*bought*' from Namirembe Hospital, I wander down the mountain. Austere winds whisper in my ears, blowing my hair all over my face. As I independently skip, day-insects acknowledge my existence with chirps.

Once Daddy dug up a long earthworm and put in my hand, "*Never be afraid of these, Mandy. They will not harm you. They fertilize the earth.*" Nothing can harm me in *heaven*. We have nothing harmful or evil. Mr. Sunshine keeps us warm throughout the year. Only when God goes to sleep behind blackened mountains does the world freeze. That's when Helene, Daddy and I cuddle up in front of a crackling fireplace listening to mighty thunderous rain and watch lightening at intervals. Our kerosene light quivers from slight wind. Daddy makes funny figures on the wall with his hands and I roll over on the mat in a paroxysm of hilarity.

Before Daddy had money for a stone house we lived in the depth of the forest in mud huts. We awoke with the variety of birds twittering querulously, larger ones flew off complaining about my presence. Sad to say these naughty mummy birds leave birdies with wide open mouths crying for food.

Daddy had once lifted me up to show me a nest. Cute, bearded monkeys peered at us, screeching. At night with wild dogs baying at the moon, distant blood-curdling laughter of hyenas, evil wild cats, leopards and lions lurking around terrified us so we tightly cuddle next to Mummy.

Every morning I hear invisible mothers humming to babies snuggled on bare backs and echoes of men's laughter. The same small structured men, scatter like army red ants I once disturbed on an anthill. Mummy is always busy: crocheting socks for us, patching Daddy's khaki shorts, darning his socks, cooking, or feeding baby Sylvia.

When I see so many people I ask Daddy how much is a hundred. Daddy spreads my ten fingers out. *"Multiply ten by ten you get one hundred. Multiply that by three you get three hundred."* That is confusing but I promise to work at it. As I examine some insects, Daddy cautions me to be careful. I might get stung. I

4

have to watch out for snakes and even nettles. A big black beetle zooms across my face scaring the daylight out of me. We laugh. Life is funny.

At end of each month, I watch Daddy distribute a ration of imperishable foods to the workers. On receiving paper money they sign off with a thump print in an oblong, black covered book; always showing Daddy gratitude. Daddy explains when I grow up and have a job I will be paid likewise, but *I* will sign a signature. As shops are inaccessible in our world, Daddy buys a months' supply of food and other essential and stocks them in a pantry. Our nearest town, Kabale is about seventy-five miles away; run by white and Indian people. Being a hazard, long trip Daddy advises me, *"Better stay with Mummy."* Life isn't that bad. I have my baby, Sylvia, and big sister Helene to play with.

Uncle Sverre and Aunt Liv, work for Daddy. I have a girl-cousin, Svanhild. When Mummy visits Grandma without us we sometime spend the daytime with our cousin. I sneak off to mountain mothers only because they offer me sorghum and millet food. I am forbidden to eat such. Mummy, who is part Arab and part an African princess, exempted us eating from commoners. I am proud to say Grandma and Mummy have seen King George and his wife Elizabeth, when they visited Uganda. Posters of them are in every home and hut.

Despite Mummy's warnings about not begging food from other people that did not stop Helene from pleading for chewing gum from a child at Sverre's. The child mischievously says, *shut your eyes and open your mouth and I'll pop one into your mouth.* Helene obediently does as instructed and *the child* spat into in her mouth! To avoid a spanking we kept it a secret.

5

Had Daddy found out he would go berserk and furiously shouted about *the contaminations of spittle?* Like Howard Hughs, Daddy is paranoid about germs.

When darkness falls shadowy fissures in the cliffs appear, trees branches begin entwining above my head; I run up a serpentine footpath back home to safety. The servants carry hot water in tin buckets and quarter fill a ceramic big bath. As Daddy baths me he tells me wonderful tales about his country Norway. If there was anything I loved most about Daddy was his deep baritone voice. His people, the Scandinavian, travelled as far as America and became farmers in Wisconsin and Minnesota. Since pronouncing Bjordal is difficult, Africans gave Daddy pet names.

"I am called Kanya Mugara sometimes Kanwa Musoke," Daddy informs me.

As we eat Norwegian tinned herrings, Daddy says *"Lovely fish. Even hundreds of Norwegian escapees to England never forgot to carry smoked herrings hidden in their luggage."* Years later, Daddy told me that during the Wars, hundreds of Norwegians families escaped to England. Despite the Viking hacking the British to death many years ago, the English landed in Baltasund and protected Norway. *"Mostly because of the oil."* Daddy confirmed. When Daddy was prospecting gold in Uganda in 1940, Hitler's Germany invaded Norway. I listened without really understanding what war was all about. It was my Daddy's story.

Daddy says Kabale resembles Norway. Pointing at an opposite hill, we watch mountain men terrace the land. This prevents soil erosion. Heavy rains deplete it. We appreciate grand panoramas of mountain tops, with steeping descents, green hillsides, and every kind of

6

plant blooms around us throughout the year. Our days and nights are equal. Early mornings fluffy white clouds completely cover our world beneath us. I so wish to sail on them but Daddy warns me that vertiginous slopes could make me dizzy and I'd go tumbling down below. *"You wouldn't want that,"* Daddy says. I point to pure white lambs, (clouds) like cotton wool, changing shapes and disappearing beneath our very feet travelling off to taller mountains peaks: shrouding them like a thick woollen blanket. A pellucid, blue sky stays on the whole day. I sop up everything as a sponge does with water.

In the evenings when the sky redden, my once a sailor Daddy says, *"That's a sailor's delight. It predicts a lovely day."* Being alert, I try to be as competitive as Daddy and I say; when you see a smiling moon it predicts a sunny day. Actually, I learnt that from my Grandma. We both laugh as swings me around. He believes I'm ready for school.

At dinnertime, Daddy tells Mummy he wants to send us to the best school in Switzerland. I am all excited. Mummy seems shocked but says nothing. Early next day, we *have to* visit Grandma at the royal hill of Mengo. Daddy takes us to Kabale and hires a taxi. On either sides of the road are thousands of distant wild animals. Despite the rough muram road and perhaps the extreme heat, I sleep most of the way arriving Kampala late in the evening.

Grandma happily enfolds us in her outstretched arms and endlessly fusses over us. Next day, Mummy seeks advice from the Kattikiro, a chief in-charge of Mengo. Rumours in East Africa said, eventually, white men take their African babies abroad never to be seen again.

7

"Your husband might have ulterior motives. Being royalty makes no difference to a white man, really," a higher chief resolutely advises Mummy in court.

I could not fathom why Mummy did this to *my* Daddy? How often had she left us alone with him when she visited Grandma and found us safe and sound?

I believe there was a court case and Mummy was given full custody. My life ended there and then.

"Smile for Daddy, Mandy" – 1945

CHAPTER TWO
THE REAL WORLD

Well, I now live in Kampala after dropping from a cool *heaven* down to an unreasonably hot, busy, noisy, dusty city. Millions and millions of people, like safari ants, aimlessly mill around. Car-fumes make me sick.

However, Mummy is proud of me. Amongst her children, I am the dancer and the singer. *How I danced, sang and was a chatter-box in heaven.* She calls me to dance for her friends. No one in this world could hold a candle toward me and make shine. Grandma realizes my unhappiness and takes me out for walks.

"*Jajja, the water here is brown and floating with rubbish,*" I complain as we cross a stream near the *Lubiri,* palace. I explain to Jajja that in *heaven* we scooped up blue water from running rivers, cascading down waterfalls, into cupped palms and drank it when thirsty. I cannot do that here even if I am dying of thirst. Daddy said dirty water carries *dudus,* parasites and virus making people very, very ill. I do not want to be confined in bed or hospital. Up the mountain, Daddy boils or filters water adding a drop or two of Milton. I furtively had a little taste of it. Yak! It was very salty. No wonder it kills those, *dudu.*

"*My child, the Muzungu exaggerates about little things. How did Africans survive if we did not take care about our health? Look at them dying of malaria, typhoid, and dysentery! They should consult my mother. She cures all those diseases,*" Grandma tells me.

I am four years, this August of 1949. My aunt Liv has had a baby girl, Berit. I do remember this quite clearly: a bundled up pink baby. Together with two

9

year old sister Sylvia, we explore Grandma's plantain, shady garden. Elsewhere is hot like Daddy's bake-oven. Helene is nowhere to be seen.

Although Namirembe is hilly, it is nothing in comparison to Daddy's *heaven*. People here stare at us like we come from outer space, mournfully saying, *bambi*, why are you sad? If you have never met a more frowning, sour looking child you should have met me. It's no wonder people and family said I wasn't as pretty as my siblings. *"Don't you know I want my Daddy?"* I shout at them in Luchiga, a language they didn't understand.

Not knowing what the word *Bambi* meant I ask Grandma about it. She smiles and explains; *bambi* means cute or poor thing in the Luganda language depending on the situation. Oh well, I better make friends with Baganda children and teach them Luchiga. The silly children only giggle and tease me as being *Omungeleza,* English. Grandma corrects them that *my* Daddy is *not* English but a Norwegian. So we are termed as *Banowe.* Years later, Grandma told me that the Dutch, Germans, Portuguese and Italians did horrible things in other parts of Africa. *Muslims in Mombasa or Zanzibar are good to their slaves,* she said. Whenever Baganda Kings won tribal wars they took on slaves from the loosing tribe and sold them to Arab traders. I was proud Grandma grew up in Zanzibar Island she knew what was talking about. On the other hand, I did not comprehend this weird story about *watumwa,* slaves.

I often chose Grandma over Mummy. I guess she replaced Daddy. Mummy later told me that as early as six months old I'd screech and clutch on Grandma

10

when she tried to take me back. She often left me with grandma being rocked to sleep.

Passersby often kneel before Grandma in greeting. Although I am confused, I realize she must be a special woman. A princess. Being exempted from physical work passersby offer to babysit me but being extremely protective Grandma does not let them touch me. Mummy, on the other hand, lets everyone hold me; something I did not like at all. It's a great privilege working for royalties. If Grandma needs extra men with various chores she asks the King Mutesa II, and he sends five or ten prisoners to help her. I make friends with these happy and friendly men enjoying good lunches from Grandma. I wonder why they dress alike in khaki outfits and have shaven, shiny heads. As I thoughtfully look at them, Grandma ushers me to keep my distance. These men are naughty and are being punished. Daddy never did that to people at the mine.

Whenever Uncle Sverre Henrik and Aunty Liv make a trip to Kampala; they visit us bringing lots of food and all sorts of goodies. On one of those visits, I caused such havoc when they were about to leave. I hid in the backseat determine not to be left behind. *I have to see my Daddy.* Uncle Sverre laughs asking Mummy permission to take me back to Daddy.

Hurray. I am back in *heaven* with Daddy! Mountain people welcome me back with staccato laughter. All mother animals have wiggly kids, calves, and puppies. As I approach them, mother goat complains with baas, the cow moos and the bitch barks at me. Daddy says I dare not hold their babies otherwise I'll be butted, kicked or snapped at. Strange as it may sound, I had missed the smoky smell of mountain inhabitants, animals, plants and the earth when touched with

11

insidious drizzle. Daddy baths and dresses me warmly before dinnertime. Time to sleep; my forehead is gently rubbed as I dreamily hear about, Olaf Tryggvason, king of Norway. Olaf was only a baby, when he lost his father, Trygg, in a battle. His mother escaped with him first to Germany and later to England. The wicked Queen Gunhild and King Ear Hakoron wanted them arrested. Norwegian pirates attacked the ship and took Olaf and sold him as a slave.

In the meantime, elders questioned Mummy how could she give her baby to a white man? Did she think about what the uncultured Bachiga people might do to me? What if I wandered off on my own and a wild animal killed me?

Not long after Mummy unexpectedly turned up at the Mine and took me away amidst struggles and screams. I watched my redden-faced Daddy tearfully see me go. Totally distraught, I drift off to sleep sniffling away in the taxi. Thereafter, I developed thumb-sucking, my greatest comforter.

This was the time Daddy drove to Mombasa to get over his misery. He met an exotic Australian dancer woman, Marjory, and married her within that short stay.

Daddy was twenty six when he married my seventeen year old mother. Ulfhild was twenty one and Daddy was thirty eight years old when they lived together. I'm not sure the age of Marjory.

Now, at four years old, I crouch at the roadside watching every car that passes by expecting that one of those white, blonde men might be my Daddy. I wave at them, praying they'd stop and I'd ask them where my Daddy was.

My perturbed mind was distracted when Mummy dropped me at her sister at Namirembe. She actually slyly went off with Helene and Sylvia leaving me behind with her strict, childless sister crying my heart out. Anyway, after a week, she came back with this beautiful, fat baby born March 1950. We spent some time with her sister getting help before going back home to Nankulyabe. Two years later Uncle Sverre had the cutest African baby daughter Emily. Her mother showed us a photograph in 1954.

Heart-broken Daddy had been alone two months when he remembered Mummy left pregnant and rushed to Kampala. Can you imagine my joy seeing Daddy in person? He overlooked me as he fussed over his new baby.

"She shall be called Berit a family name," he smiled. Liv and her babies left for good in 1949. I met another cousin Berit daughter of Daddy's sister Aasluag in 1966. In October of 1950, Daddy received shocking news of a son, Raymond David, born October 7th at Rose Park Hospital in Australia nine months later! Marjory was sure this would bring her husband over to Australia or at least attend the Baptism on 25th November that year. Daddy never did. Instead, a divorce and child support was arranged. Daddy supported an unknown son to his dying day 1969. In 1952, for some unknown reasons Daddy and Sverre had some misunderstanding and they physically fought. Uncle Sverre lay very ill in bed wheezing terribly for a week. Realizing the seriousness of the situation, Daddy drove him three hundred miles to Mulago Hospital. X-rays revealed three broken ribs almost touching his lungs. Sverre was hospitalized for a long time. Daddy brought Uncle Sverre all bandaged up to say goodbye. I was rather concerned about what might have happened but did not questioned Daddy. On leaving Uganda, I

13

believe, Uncle Sverre married a different Norwegian mummy; probably a nurse or a Norwegian volunteer he met in Kampala. Perhaps their story has a different version. The adult world is full of mysteries and confusion. I could not keep up with them.

In 1951, there was great excitement. A big stone house was being built for us down Namirembe Hill. Living three hundred miles away from Kampala, Daddy entrusted a one-eyed constructor, Kamya. Thinking of it now he may have had a cataract.

Daddy travelled to Norway. I might have heard that his mother had died. During this visit to Norway, he returned with twenty one year old beauty, Ulfhild. Later on, as I watched Dynasty series, in my mind's eye, I found Ulfhild resembled Linda Evans, a blonde American actress. At first, I thought Ulfhild was Daddy's secretary because she did our shopping. Daddy carried all sorts of boxes into our Aunt's house. I walked up to the car and said *Jambo*, hello to Ulfhild. I thought she might come out of the car and cuddle me as most adults did but she overlooked me staying put in the car. As usual the weather was steaming hot.

More changes took place thereafter. In 1952, arrangements were made for us to go into a Catholic Boarding School. Helene will turn eight in May, I six in August, and Sylvia four in March. I heard rumours that Daddy's new wife wanted to limit his visits at our home. Well, it turned out right. We saw Daddy less and less.

A wonderful nun, Sister Mary John, drove us in a car to the school. What a privilege that was. Every weekend Mummy and Grandma visited us. They were thoroughly impressed with this spotless school; excited that we were to be educated and be morally and

14

physically nurtured. No more worries for Mummy taking us to a classy Goan School on public transport up another hill. I remember only two visits from Daddy at the school, after Mummy complained we were being mistreated by African girls. Daddy never reacted from hearsay but had to find out for himself.

Shortly, the tables turned and the mistreatments worsen beyond description. Not only that but we were attacked with measles, chicken pox, malaria and to top it off I got rheumatic fever and asthma. My little life was filled with fear watching children caned. I had never seen such things in my *heaven.* I too was unjustly whipped at that school as mentioned in my first book Where Do We Belong. Had I taken Daddy's advice of being bold, honest and speaking up perhaps that would not have happened. I did not scream, only chokingly whimpered, "*I want my Daddy,*" rubbing my aching thighs and legs. Unseen pressure was lifted off my head every time I was away from this environment. Daddy visited me and showed me a photograph of our new brother, Haakon, born end of December 1952. Another very pale brother, Braaken, was born in October 1953 eleven months later.

"*How can you have other children when you have us,*" I wanted to ask Daddy as I did not understand what was going on. At the end of 1954, after I recovered from a combination of rheumatic and typhus fevers I heard whispers that my sisters were smuggled to Kenya. Missing Daddy and now my sisters, was *the* most unnatural blow I had to deal with for two years of my life. Unable to express my inner feelings to family members I talked to my brain. Probably the asthma attacks expressed my emotional sufferings. However, grandma filled the gap by overly pampering me. When

15

she was in Kampala there I was comforted on her laps or her back. When she travelled to Kenya there I was smothered in a coal smoking train jutting out of a chimney snaking in and out hills. Business-minded Grandma owned a house with a complex of rented out rooms in Shauri Moyo, managed by her mother, Nattimba. Grandma collected accumulated rent and became rich and independent. Grandma's character was such that we defiantly walked into a *White Only,* New Stanley Hotel and waited to be served. African waiters nervously stationed around us uncertain whether this African woman was a nanny: patiently waited to see my white parents.

Grandma was the only African educated in a *White Only* St Monica's school in Zanzibar. She politely requested for the menu in the Queens' English, which I hardly knew. The nervous waiters ignored her. She walked to the manager's office asked why *she* a princess of Buganda was not attended to, warning him that if we were not immediately served she'd walk straight to Lord Delamere's office. To my surprise, as we enjoyed the English tea, Grandma expounded horrible things the English did to Africans. *"They are mistreating Africans right here in their own country."* Uninterested, I asked her if we were to visit my sisters. *"With my skin colour? Impossible. Moreover, I'm in the nun's black book!"* she said. Nuns in Mangu were on guard against this dangerous Muslim woman whose father King Mwanga II killed Christians. Much as it was against the English policy, they respected the Baganda royal family. Therefore we ate at Norfolk and Windsor hotels without problem. At this tender age my mind was jumbled up, troubled and confused about discrimination. My Daddy was never mean to Africans.

16

He treated Grandma, Aunt, and my Great Grandma with respect. I wanted to ask him if other white people are naturally born mean and wicked to people of colour? "*In Kenya, the whites do*", he'd say. I asked Grandma why my sisters did not come home. She said Kenya was in a state of emergency due to the Mau Mau, a Kikuyu tribal group. Not only were the whites killed but Africans who corroborated with them. They were given no choice. No wonder I suffer so much from head pains. Such things never existed where I came from.

Could these English tell Daddy not to love me? Did they kidnap my siblings? Seeing me bored, Grandma sent me outside to play with children who spoke only Kikuyu, calling me a *Mukoloni*, a colonialist. My brain told me Grandma does not want me snooping around listening to adult discussing serious issues.

In Uganda I cannot play with *my* baby sister Berit. She is too small, heavy and fussy. I hated Mummy overdressing me to stop nosey friends asking if I had tuberculosis. You get very thin with that disease. As it is; it's steaming hot here in Kampala. I had none of this when I was with Daddy. I was my own boss up in the mountains. Now I want to scream at everyone. I talked a lot to my brain in 1950 before falling asleep. I asked Helene if does likewise. She laughed at me and said, "NO, Silly." After a long time Daddy visited us. Mummy told him about my troubled chest. He rested me on a bed and gently rubbed my forehead encouraging me to relax. My arms were lifted and dropped. "*You will soon fall into a deep, deep sleep at the count of ten. And when you wake up you will never wheeze again.*" Daddy said in Kiswahili. Daddy later spoke of being gifted in hypnotism. Much later in life

17

he suggested hypnosis to Ulfhild. She underrated him. As far as I am concerned my Daddy is a great Doctor. I know one day he will cure me.

Daddy visited Helene and Sylvia in Kenya at a remote school thirty seven miles from Nairobi in a white Chevrolet. Probably Ulfhild and babies stayed behind at the Norfolk hotel. Looking at the photograph I saw my sisters alone at this huge school holding thick coats and dressed in uniforms. Kenya gets cold from June to August. I envied them getting an education whilst I sat at home bored to death. I wondered why Mummy never visited them.

I wanted to tell Daddy, my heart beats weird at times; it goes fast then misses a few beats. When I told Mummy about it we walked up hill to Mengo Hospital. Dr. Billington checked me with a weird instrument called stethoscope.

"She is fine. I do not feel anything out of the ordinary," the doctor confirmed. Daddy randomly mentioned an aspirin was good for the heart. That inspired me to buy aspirin and sucked one or two twice a day. I loved the sourly taste. I believe Aspirins made the pain go away. Don't ask me how I have cents or how I sneak up the hill to a convenient shop in Mengo despite hating the brilliant steaming sun. Since taking ill, I do not see very well and my skin is sensitive to heat. Nothing I say will make the doctor or Mummy believe me. They think it's my imagination. Only Daddy believes me. If I complain about pain, *which is rare*, I'm either told to lie down or go play outside. When a child complains of pain parents should listen to them. Not only does the *wheezing,* worsens when I lay down but a maddening drone of mosquitoes bite me all night long. I hate the DDT Mummy sprays every

evening. The smell increases the coughing. Sometimes I cough so much I throw up phlegm. Mummy says that is good. It clears my congested lungs. Without Daddy: the dark hours, sounds of flapping curtains, the clattering and thumping of strange things when heavy rains fall frighten me. More so because Mummy and Grandma are terribly afraid of sky activities and call upon God, *Allah aw-kubhar.'* Daddy made me listen to echoes of thunder and look at the lightning in the brightening skies at intervals. It was fun. Now I am told thunder and lightning are angry gods. Maybe these gods took my sisters. Sylvia and I were like two peas in a pod. I mostly keep alone; busy with my brain. Daddy had said the brain is your best friend. If you use it correctly, it will guide you.

As an adult I met a Greek man who told me, "*Your father was miserable when your Mama took you away. I've not known a man who loved his children as your father loved you.*" This Greek man had visited Norway and had accidently met a teenage Haakon. Looking at me he continued, "*This is unbelievable. The only difference between your brother Haakon and you is the colour of the skin and hair. You have the same teeth and smile.*"

Unfortunately, when I was little I had no way to express myself. All I could think of was to *scream for all I was worth. Give hell to the person who is messing with my life!* I wished Mummy, my Jajja and Aunt asked me what *I* wanted. I was capable of making choices at a young age. I was four years old for-crying-out-loud. Even babies cry when they want something or when another person, other their mother holds them.

One thing I am certain of is that Daddy would never let us out of his *castle* to sleep over at friend's or even at his brother Sverre's home. He made sure we were safe up there in his castle, when he went down the mountain to work. Of course, I sneaked away to be with mountain people, the only other inhabitants I saw. They belonged to me.

On leaving Daddy I wanted to tell Mummy; *"Please, please Mummy leave me with Daddy."* I am sure I would have been OK with stepmother and brothers with visits to Kampala. Despite restrictions Daddy never gave up on us. Even with the circumstances that existed in East Africa. I admired Daddy for that. Beautiful young Ulfhild knew about us, before plunging herself in Africa. She made a choice. Like any African in East Africa, Mummy would never trust us with this colonial woman. *Bibi mudogo,* second wife as referred to in Kiswahili. Awful accidents do happen to stepchildren even today 2014.

Once in 1954, a total stranger, took me to Nairobi to visit Grandma. Chugging along in third class on wooden benches sitting up the whole night some four hundred miles from Uganda to Kenya my stomach turned tipsy-turvey and I threw up on passengers in front of me. Newspapers and head clothes were used to clean me up. I became watchful and protective.

My beautiful, esteemed Mummy's *people* are sophisticated, clean, always elegantly dressed unlike *my* people up in *heaven,* with just a blanket thrown over naked bodies. How else should I feel or think when I do not belong here? My Uncle Sverre and family lived sort of the middle of this mountain; somewhere like where my heart is. Workers were at the lower end of the mountain below where my feet are. Everything in my *heaven is connected to me.* At least that's what I thought. Because Daddy made me aware of the importance of school since small, I had several tug-of-wars about that with Mummy. Frustrated with my determination and persistence, Mummy sent me to five different schools, one Indian home, one Goan girl for private tuition in two years 1954-1955 including home tuition in Arabic writing and the Koran.

Mummy said, "*Since you are so smart complaining about every school I send to, you might as well run a convenient shop.*" Mind you, I couldn't read or write. I assumed only white people, Arabs and Indians do. I had no choice but to comply.

When I got a customer I added and subtracted in my friend, *brain,* as Mummy had instructed me to. I recorded money transaction in a given black hard covered book using strokes like a prehistoric man. Doing business was the most boring experience I ever had.

An old, old man, Ganafa with long beard shimmering like mercury running down his stomach, flying all over when the spirit wind angrily blew caught my attention. On noticing me, Ganafa ushered me over to his hut and gave me a local alcoholic drink *Gwete* in a tattered tin bowl. Taking a sip, it travelled straight to my head. I stumbled, reeling over with laughter. Ganafa wickedly cackled. That was not a good thing to do. No wonder Mummy strictly warned me not to step out of the shop or talk to strangers. Going back to my business the earth beneath my feet trembled. I thought it must be the drink. Mummy rushed to save me saying her ancestors' spirits were angry the British whisked the King, Mutesa II to England. When I later learnt Shakespeare's Shylock, I figured he must have looked like Ganafa. What a bizarre world we live in.

21

Uncle Sverre and Aunt Liv

Camila and Kristoffer, Sverre's great grandchildren

Cousin Svanhild and her daughters

CHAPTER THREE
DADDY SENDS ME TO KENYA

January nineteen fifty-six was the start of the best year of my life. Daddy finally sent me to a school that loved strange creatures like me in colonial Kenya. Daddy said that white sisters arrived in Kenya in 1907 much before the British. These French nuns, led by Mother Majella, rode on a donkey for over thirty-seven miles to Mangu. Finding Mangu fertile, they planted coffee, an orchard and physically built a stone church and convent. The English, Indians and Arabs were well established with schools, prayer places and hospitals for their own communities. Realizing that children of mixed parentage were marginalized, the nuns decided to open a school for such children. We had German-mix from Tanganyika (Tanzania) and English, Italians and Norwegian mix from Uganda, English, Scottish, Greek mix from Kenya, Seychellois and Goans. Going to this English country, Kenya, was like going abroad. I am sure Daddy heard my thanks in the wind as he and Ulfhild sipped tea at the very verandah where he and I watched the moon and stars and blackened mountains.

Our school had children from age six to seventeen, some a little older. You spent seven years in the primary school up to age thirteen then spent four years in the secondary school; if you are lucky. We had one girl who made it to the Royal University, Nairobi. Our system was very much British unlike America with pre-school, kindergarten, middle school and high school.

I was assigned an identification number of 175. My sisters were 72 and 74, if I remember correctly.

23

I painted beautiful scenes hoping to be given, at least, one artwork to show my Daddy but the nuns pinned up my work in the hall. I wondered if Ulfhild would let me visit *my heaven* in Kigezi when the holidays come. I honestly never liked Mengo, Namirembe or Kampala. As for foreign Kenya it will always be my second home. Many men here resemble Daddy.

I go back and forth Kenya and Uganda every April, August and December with my sisters for term holidays. Mummy and Helene cry every departure but not Sylvia and me. I love school and the white women dressed in long white gowns. Doesn't Helene realize this *is a better school than Kisubi?* Oh well, I let her figure it out. She is such a sweet big sister, so kind and loving. I would not have survived without her. Imagine we are only two years apart, for Pete sake. *"God please bless my sister Helene,"* I often pray.

The first time I was to leave for the boarding school, I was so anxious for the train to start fearing Mummy might change her mind and take me back home to rest. I was sick and tired being treated like an invalid.

We squashed at the narrow corridor whilst a uniformed man made our beds with light, crispy bed sheets. I liked the smell of the upholstery, the clacking of the wheels, the chugging and wailing of the locomotive and rhythmic sway of the berth. In no time they put me to sleep.

Next morning, unobserved by Sister Bethlehem, Sylvia ushered me the 'White Only toilets.' We sat on toilet seats, used Andrex soft toilet paper and washed our hands with lavender soaps. Odd people like us and Africans squatted over a hole type toilet. Beaming red-

24

faced nuns, similar to the ones at Kisubi, met us at Nairobi Station. All eyes riveted on me in the school bus pointing at my freckled face and touching my straight blonde hair. Everything about me seemed odd. Once an Indian doctor, Ganatra, said to Mummy, *"Your daughter would have been a pretty girl if not of these freckles."* I wanted to tell him, *"Who cares, I look like my Daddy. His body is covered with them."* Luckily, my sisters have lovely even-colour complexions. Sylvia proudly introduced me to her little freckled, thumb-sucking friend, a duplicate of me. Unlike me, she was outrageously mischievous. We bonded like a hand wearing a glove as we both spoke Kiswahili.

On arrival, my eyes widen on seeing this huge double storied school in person which Daddy had shown me in photographs in 1954. The white walls were spotless and the floors sparkling. I was excited about the variety of hot meals. For breakfast we had either porridge or slices of baked bread with homemade butter. I will never forget the bowls of *cold UJI,* the corn porridge every day, symmetrically placed on wooden benches under two mango trees at Kisubi. I was taught to scoop out fat white worms with a leaf or finger. We immediately learned the meaning of survival.

I slept up in a clean attic with a blue light on throughout the night. This helped find the pail to relief ourselves. Older girls used flash toilets at night on the first floor.

Full-fledged nightmares bothered me every night. *"Tell Daddy what the children do to us, Mandy,"* Helene sternly ordered me. *"Show him the blisters on your hand."* These were caused by digging in the forest that very afternoon Daddy visited us. Evidence of abuse

25

was right there on our hands! Tough as Daddy was, he could not bear any child mistreated. He could easily have blamed himself for not listening to Mummy about the bullying at Kisubi. Had he found me in the terrible condition I was in, he would have called the police or opened a court case against the school.

"What the hell are you doing to my children? How did these blisters form on their little hands?" Daddy's voice woke me up and I ran to pee.

Up to his death, we never told Daddy the hell we went through.

Taking me to the White Sister School was an overwhelming experience for me, like a prisoner set free. Reading about tortured Jews later on in life they had a place in my heart.

Hardly had three weeks passed when a constant thought of writing to my Daddy pestered me. I persevere boring handwriting practices during playtime. Having done nothing, but fleet in and out five different schools for the past two years, I did not mind the tedious work! Moreover I was least interested in games, using every precious moment to master this tricky English language. When defeated I timidly asked a kindly Maasai-English girl in Kiswahili; *tafadhali, nisaidie kwandika burua kwa babagu,* please help me write a letter to my Daddy. Sitting beside Gracie, I dictated the letter in Kiswahili and she drafted it into English

White Sisters Convent,
Thika,
20th February 1956

Dear Daddy,

How are you? As for me, I am well thank you. I can speak English. I can write in English. I like school.

I like the White Sisters. I like my teacher Miss Hooker. She is pretty. When I am baptized next year, I have to give up my pagan name Mandy and take a Saint's name Margaret. Helene gave me that good Catholic name. Sylvia and Helene will be Catholics in June.

Thank you for sending me to Thika. I love you very much.

Your loving Daughter,
Mandy

A month later, a bell rang summoning us to line up according to our dormitory with the shortest girl at front going upwards to the tallest last. I was fourth in line somewhere at the centre. *Miss Bjordal,* the nun called, searching for me in the crowd. I stretched my skinny neck with anticipation. *"Come along Margaret,"* I was encouraged. Squealing with joy I ran up the stairs.

My Daddy had written! Yes, indeed. I love you, I love you Daddy. I impolitely grabbed an already opened letter from the nun.

"Remember your manners, Miss Bjordal," Sister Mary De Lorette said looking at me above her thick glasses.

Years later Daddy told me, *"You know Mandy; during the wars in Europe the Nazi prisoners of war received unopened letters. I do not understand the daringness of the nuns reading my letters before you do!* Well, I suppose that's what Holy people do. I never trusted anyone but Daddy.

Bjordal Mine Limited
Kabale, Uganda,
28th February 1956

My Dear Daughter,

27

I cannot believe you can already write so beautifully? Your hand writing, English grammar and spellings are all correct. Good for you, Mandy, I am so proud of you. I gave you a beautiful English name. Who says its pagan?

Perhaps Sister Mary de Lorette reads your letters because she wants to help you with spelling mistakes and English grammar before sending your letters home.

Give my love to Helene and Sylvia

Your loving,

Daddy

Running to my new friend with my Daddy's letter I ask her to tell me what he had written. Looking at the letter she said my father must be an important man like a minister to have professionally printed out envelopes. After translating Daddy's English letter into Kiswahili she said, "*From now onwards, I will print out the letter and you copy it in your own handwriting,*" seriously confirming like a real teacher would.

That was great! I copied what she wrote in my best handwriting and handed an open letter to the nun. I felt guilty deceiving Daddy and worse still being praised for making such quick progress. So I diligently worked hard to be self-sufficient.

Much against my inner oppositions, the nuns continued reading my letters for the next nine years.

Come April holidays Daddy kissed and hugged me, "*I knew you would do it, Mandy,*" he said proudly.

My mind had recorded unusual happenings at the school, but revealing them to our parents was a sin; needing confession, you know. So, I reserved everything at the back of my mind. Things like: Sylvia secretly taking me outside a storeroom where an ugly, tall, skinny man whipped children who wetted their

28

beds whilst asleep or Sylvia incarcerated in cold, blinding underground cellars used for storing suitcases. She often encountered rats. Daddy had said, *"If you are ever bitten by a rat, you get infected with the deadly plague."* I never liked rats or bees. I never knew what Sylvia did in absolute darkness. Did she sing? Pray the rosary? Plan an escape? Say her favourite poems by William Blake?

Infant Sorrow

My mother groaned, my father wept,
Into the dangerous world I leapt;
Helpless, naked, piping loud,
Like a fiend hid in a cloud.
Trudging in my father's hands,
Striving against me swaddling bands,
Bound and weary, I thought best,
To sulk upon my mother's breast.

William Black.

I could not imagine what Daddy might have done had he known about these punishments. He probably would have driven from Uganda to Kenya, like a safari relay driver, and made hell in the school. On the whole, little ones were well taken for. I truly loved this school.

My nightmares of Kisubi continued many a night. Grandma once forgot to give us the lovely milky toffees when she visited us. She walked back to the school and literally budged in the teacher's house. Hell broke loose when she found them eating our food. She almost choked them. This dream often wakes me up and I run to pee in the bucket placed under a dim blue and fall back to sleep.

29

Daddy showed me a photo of my Norwegian baby brothers, Haakon and Braaken seated on either side of him high up in my *heaven*. I guess Daddy is happy with them because he's smiling. Maybe if I were a boy I'd have been with him.

"How old are they?" I ask Daddy in Kiswahili when he finally visited me and took a photograph of me and my brother Frank, on my mother's side.

"One is two years and one is a year old," showing two fingers then one. I thought they were cute. I still have that photo stuck in my album but left it in Uganda when I migrated to America.

"What are their names?" I asked Daddy.

"Haakon and Braaken David."

"Their hair is white Daddy," I commented observing the photograph.

"It's called blonde, Mandy. Yours is ash blonde." Daddy smiled nuzzling my hair.

Daddy explained that Ulfhild used a yellow liquid called *Light and Bright*. That keeps blonde hair from darkening. Daddy promised to get me a bottle in the next shopping trip. It smelt good too unlike undulated coconut oil Mummy used on us. After Ulfhild took over our shopping Light and Bright was replaced with Brylcreem. That was good too. Daddy said it was rather oily. I envied Helene and Sylvia's lovely, thick, soft curls.

I have vivid memories when Daddy first brought Ulfhild to visit us, in nineteen-fifty-one. I was excited to meet his new *mummy* but she denied my existence even when I said *Jambo*. Oh well, Uncle Sverre and Aunt Liv come right indoors when they visit us. I had hoped Daddy's new mummy would do likewise but she never even touched me. For the next nine years, Ulfhild never visited us nor let us see our brothers.

Beaming Daddy came home with our reports in 1956 overjoyed I was ranked sixth out of over twenty six children. This time I was able to sit right next to Daddy, stroking his hairy arms; a habitual trend of mine since childhood. It was taboo in our Baganda and Arabic culture. Moreover I am eleven years old now. The nuns at Kisubi distant us, as well, when Daddy visited in 1953. We sat on chairs arranged directly opposite him, closer to the nun. How I wished to be cuddled in Daddy's arms but I understood where my place was. Was I normal wanting Daddy's affection? Always choosing Daddy over anyone? My fun Daddy seemed changed and uptight. Hardly had a half hour passed when he looked at his watch. He is expected back at the Grand Hotel he tells the nun. My honest Daddy never lies. I therefore comforted myself that Daddy's short visits were *better than none at all.* Once I am fluent in English, I shall come out of my reverie and express my thoughts to *my* Daddy.

Well, obstacles came and I never did.

White Sisters School,
Thika, Kenya,
28th January 1957

Dear Daddy,

I am so happy in grade four. Sylvia beats me in every subject but I am proud to have such a clever sister. She helps me when she has time to spare; otherwise, she is on the move non-stop. I cannot keep up with her as I tire easily.

Mother Miriam from Kisubi, whom you know very well, takes good care of me when I get asthma attacks. I love her. She once asked me why was I sickly and I said the nuns in Kisubi made me so. She told me nuns do not do that. A wonderful teacher, Miss Hooker, has moved me up to the front row because I cannot see the Blackboard.

Your loving daughter,

Margaret

I do not remember letters from Daddy from February to March.

Some friends secretly told me their fathers had white wives and children abroad. I comforted myself with the fact that Mummy was Daddy's first wife. Another little friend giggled and said her father was a priest and her mother was a novice but she left the convent to have her. I did not believe her. Priests aren't supposed to have a Mummy. Being very mischievous she must be pulling my leg but she signed herself with the cross and swore it was true.

"Don't take God's name in vain," I warned her. "*Oh well, I shall ask Daddy if this is true.*" Slowly but surely I began to learn a little about deception.

Like any child, I forgot to ask Daddy

Bjordal Mine Limited,
Kabale,
5th May 1957

My dear Daughter,

Did you give your letter to Sister Mary de Lorette to read? Well she wrote at end of your letter that she will take you at the Browse Optician in Nairobi. I am glad this school takes care of you more than Kisubi did. You will soon see clearly. Do not give up P. E altogether. You have to try; it will help you become stronger.

Now do not worry about who beats you in what subject. Do the best for yourself. I know schooling is always competitive but just work your level best and

32

you will get there. I had to do that when I was young. I am glad you are to be baptized and make your First Holy Communion. I too had to do that when I was a young boy.

Love you,
Daddy

From morning to night fall, I heard nothing but a bell ringing: at six in the morning, at break-time, at lunch time, at recess time, at benediction time, at dinner time and finally at bedtime. I mumbled prayers in English or Latin without knowing what I was saying. I cannot complain; this school is fun. *What would Daddy think about me praying so much?* I never found out.

Holy Family School
Thika
15th June 1957

Dear Daddy,

How are you? Thank you for your letter. It is now very cold in June. I'm learning Latin, Daddy. *Pater* means father, *mater* is mother, *ex tribu* means tribe. I was baptized on twenty-ninth of May and my *Eucharism Suscept,* First Holy Communion was on thirtieth of May. These two days are the greatest days of my life. I wish you had seen me dressed in a long white dress and a veil. Helene was so proud of me. Sylvia just smiled. Sister Mary asked me why I did not have lovely curly hair like my sisters.

She struggled to pin the veil on my head but it kept slipping off. Anyway, I am happy. We had a party. Sylvia and Helene sat on either side of me. The parents of the communicants were invited. Were you invited, Daddy? I know Mother could not come because she is a Muslim. She could have come for the party.

Your loving daughter, Margaret Mary

I don't remember whether or not Daddy replied. Perhaps he was out of the country. Perhaps Ulfhild didn't think it necessary travelling to Kenya for just a weekend. This was a very precious time of my life. I longed for my Daddy when I saw other fathers fussing over their little angles. My Muslim Mummy made it very clear that she was not allowed to attend Catholic ceremonies. I understood obedience to rules. She could at least come and waited outside the church. Oh well, never mind. Jesus is now my very best friend.

Sunday afternoons we often went to the woods and played hide and seek. Sundays are such fun. At four o'clock, teatime, we got a piece of home-baked cake. It tasted weird, like Lux soap. My friends informed me that the cooks used too much baking powder.

Helene and Sylvia, unfortunately, gave up music due to the music teacher's attitude. That did not deter me from learning the piano, beaten or not. I would do anything to please Daddy. He was thrilled with my decision.

"*Music teaches one discipline, patience, perseverance and broadens one's mind,*" he said encouragingly. Many students went through tension, extensive fright, and some failed due to nervousness.

I bravely sat beside a severe-looking English inspector from England or the Royal University music department and did my exam. The school was pin-point silent during that week. We were tested on the following: oral, written, sight-reading a completely new piece of music we had never learnt and played boring, major and minor, scales. A book was placed over your hands so you would not look at the keys.

Many a time our music teacher hit me in the face with the music book. It was nerve-racking and

34

humiliating but *I was determined to play the piano even if it kills me!*

I once tried sneaking a letter to Daddy, listing my complaints. Unfortunately, the Headmistress caught me red-handed and took me to the office for a lecture. I was severely warned never to write wicked things about the music teacher. Believe you me; I never did the next six years I was at the school. Instead I consistently went down a dark, eerie, stale-smelling dungeon (basement) signing myself with the cross when I heard the creaking stairs. Girls warned me of dead nuns' ghosts hovering and watching behind me when I practised.

That's where you first practise on this ancient piano. Its dark beige, hard to press keys are quite off-tune. I believe the nuns built these dungeons, (basements) in case of wars. I had never seen cellars in any normal home. My curiosity sent me to ask a friendly nun about them. During European Wars, Stalin and a-devil-incarnated man named Hitler persecuted millions of Catholics in Poland, Italy and England.

"People lived in bomb shelters similar to your suitcase room. Catholics who died during the wars are now in heaven. You have to be strong for your faith my child," I am told. I vowed to die for my faith if something like that happened in Africa. The nun hugged me and said, *"Bless you my child."* I wished Daddy were here to learn this Catholic faith. Grandma disagreed when I told her what I had heard. She said more Jews were killed than the Catholics during the European Wars. The only reason why this happened was that Jews cursed themselves and their generations after killing *Nabi,* Jesus. They paid for the sins of their fathers. Maybe Daddy knows more about this. I shall ask him. He never confuses me.

35

My adorable Grandma asked me why I became a Catholic when her father King Mwanga ll killed young Catholics. I temporarily felt afraid of her as she seriously warned me to have nothing to do with the Catholic Church. Yet Pope Pius was hung up at my Aunt's house, as well, Abrahim about to slaughter his son. Even the English royal family were displayed in huts I peered into. Such things did not matter to Daddy except music, books, good health and happiness.

Oh well, I decided to accept the disapproval of foreign teachings as well as respect my African and Muslim heritage. I learnt so much about the appreciation of music through Daddy. At the convent when percussion band was introduced I already knew the names and sounds of various instruments: the violin which Mario one of our boys played, the clarinet, trombone, and trumpet. We sang so much in school.

After great improvement on the ancient piano I was promoted to a newer piano in the school parlour! The ivory keys were whiter, the sharps jet-black and the whole outlook of the black piano spotless. I saw my delighted face in it. What a privilege that was tip-toeing on the shiny floor careful not to leave footprints; I sat on a cushioned seat and played on clear, melodic key notes to my heart's content. *Half an hour only.*

Bjordal Mine Limited
Kabale,
19th January 1957

Dear Mandy,
I am so proud of you. The nuns wrote that you are doing well in music. I am sure one day you will play like Mozart or Beethoven. With determination, there is nothing one cannot do. I loved music and carried my

36

organ with me right down to South Africa. I even earned cash reward there.

Before you were born I occasionally played it at Speke Hotel and entertained people. I love art as well and I have written about my journey across the Sahara in a magazine. Doing such things broadens your mind and you will be happier within yourself. With every experience and opportunity you get in life, learn something, out of it no matter what. I have written to Sister Mary that I hope teachers are nice to you. I wish you all the luck the world can give.

Lots of love to Helene and Sylvia and self,

Daddy

Whist Daddy encouraged me; I believed teachers purposely humiliated me by asking me to read out loud. The class laughed at my erroneous pronunciations. Well that made me completely shut down. With music, I can at least respond with my voice after the teacher plays a scale or a tune. I hear Daddy's voice say, *"With determination, you will succeed in anything you want to do."* Daddy did it the thirty years he spent with the tough mining business.

Holy Family School,
Thika
26th January 1957

Dear Daddy,

How are you? I cannot read the clock up the wall because I cannot see well.

My asthma and colds increase during the cold weather. Sometimes I lay in the infirmary for a week with books to read. The children make fun of me because I don't play much. They don't understand my knees and wrists hurt. I wish I were strong like Sylvia. Helene is shy like me. I could do things for myself but

37

the nuns put me under a tall Goan girl's care. I am getting extra help in English. My mathematic is good.

Your loving daughter,

Margaret

After enjoying my music practice, I find Helene being teased by a group of bullies a distance away. I cried only because I saw her crying. I wanted to tell the girls to *leave my sister alone* but I had no guts. They were no way near my sister's beauty; calling her lovely, thick, long hair bushy. They hardly had enough hair on their head to begin with. Daddy often said Helene got the Bjordal nose which I later discovered in the Bjordal younger generations.

Bjordal Mine-limited

Kabale,

6th February 1957

Dear Mandy,

If you learn to read the time I will buy you a watch, I promise. I have also asked Sister Mary De Lorette to take you see an optician. You will be alright; you will get stronger as you grow up. Do the physical education. Maybe I will ask the nuns if they can excuse you from races and other competitive games for the time being. Do not worry about your hair. You have lovely colour hair. I am sure this girl wishes she had your colour hair. It is beautiful. I shall write to Sister Mary about this bullying.

Love to you, Helene and Sylvia.

Daddy

Daddy would do anything to get me to learn something new. And so I learnt to read the time from my friend I played duets with; the halves, quarters, past and to. The rest I figured out myself. Sister Mary was like a mother to the three of us though she was very short tempered. It was so good to feel loved. That is how I felt with my Daddy. The first nuns I met loved my father too. No parent trusted the nuns like my Daddy. If we told him our hurts and pains he immediately wrote to the nuns to watch over us. Due to Daddy's awareness, they listened to him and took me to see a very nice English optician, Mr. Browse. He had red hair, red freckles and a red moustache. With 3.5 and 3.7 lenses I was able to see individual leaves upon trees instead of a rounded green blur! After my illness in 1953, my world was no longer as beautiful as when I was with Daddy up in *heaven*. I now sit at the back of the class where I want to be. My grades improved tremendously and Sister Mary de Lorette wanted me to skip fourth grade and go to fifth. That meant being separated from Sylvia which I did not want.

Being separated from my sisters for two years made me very suspicious of nuns. They could trick me with double promotion and take my sisters to another school. I will not let that happen again. I shall keep my sisters insight.

As I listen to Sister Mary about my progress, her eyes behind thick glasses magnified, I wanted to say, *"What big eyes you have,"* as Red Riding Hood said to the wolf. I promised to go up to the next grade but the sight of Miss Belinda's look scared me even more and I ran back to my old class with ever smiling Miss Antoinette. Sylvia got told off for my sake as the nun mixed the two of us.

Bjordal Mines Limited
Kabale,
20th May 1957

20th May 1957

20th May 1957

20th May 1957

39

My dear Mandy,

I am so proud of you. Take this opportunity. Sylvia and Helene are right there with you. You can meet them after classes. I know you love one another and are very close. You girls are very dear to me, but I cannot always be there to protect you and to make decisions for you. You have to learn to have faith in yourself.

Sister Mary is right but do not stop telling me what troubles you. I want to know everything. I will ask the nuns to give you extra help if you need it. But, if you are not comfortable going up to fifth grade by all means you can stay in fourth.

> *Love to you,*
> *Helene and Sylvia,*
> *Daddy*

I thanked Daddy for the brown leather wrist band watch, promising I'd take care of it my entire life! I thanked him for the private tuition from lovely Miss Roma after dinner.

After dealing with being teased about my spoken English now it's my height. Classmates never realized I was two years older than them therefore was taller.

Being subdued at Kisubi I became an introvert for years to come. When Daddy learnt about this he later on said, *"When you recite a poem, maximize your voice and be heard, don't mumble as if you are talking to yourself."* I was shocked to be elected a class prefect.

> *Bjordal Mine limited,*
> *Kabale,*
> *10th June 1957*

My dear Daughter,

40

Do not forget what I tell you. Every opportunity in life is an advantage, towards betterment, especially where your character is concerned. Do you know what? Daddy is very proud you have been elected a class leader. Good for you, Mandy. Seize that opportunity with both hands. I am happy you liked the watch.

Now do not worry, Mandy. Just be firm but loving to the girls and I am sure they will be good to you and not give you a tough time. Trust me.

Your proud,

Daddy

I was so excited the year, 1958. Our youngest sister Berit was joining us at school. My friend, *brain,* never figured out whether Berit went to school in Kampala, or whether she was at home bored to death as I was. Character wise, Berit is outgoing and bolder than I ever was.

As always I was happy to see Daddy during the holidays. It's a chance like a diamond. So precious that I never wanted to lose those moments. From a very young age, I knew Daddy was a meticulous, fussy man. The very reason I made such drama about my appearance when he visited us when I was barely five years old.

Since colonialist came to East Africa, division of colour took place. Becoming suspicious I wanted to ask Daddy if he was a colonialist but feared it *might be a silly question.* Both my Great Grandma and Grandma assured me my Daddy was a gentleman unlike the ruthless English.

In 1954-1955 when I travelled to Kenya with Grandma she gave an outlook about the British's attitude towards Africans. I had seen how Whites in

41

Uganda respected Grandma calling her Sir, *Sebbo,* and giving her due respect as any Africans did.

"In Kenya, the English have no respect whatsoever. They forget how my nephew, the King, entertains the Queen to the maximum. Look at them now, suspiciously staring at me because I'm holding a white child's hand. Shenzi, they think you are not my, muzuguru?" complained Grandma that whites in Kenya didn't realize I was her Grandchild.

In 1956, I listened to our part German friend discussing a terrible thing called *Gestapo.* Horrible things happened to not only Jews but other white people.

One day Sylvia dragged me to meet this German priest, Lammar, because I said I was afraid of Germans.

"Don't be afraid. He will bless you. Just ask him if he killed anyone," she mischievously teased me. Not realizing her ulterior motives, I ask Father Lammar if he were a murderer. His white face turned blood-shot and he boomed *"Fru doom de Kaiver!"* Chasing us away. He was bigger and taller than even Daddy. Sylvia was dying with laughter. I kept my distance from him until my Baptism- terrified to go for confession to him.

In the meantime, every white nun at the school expanded my knowledge about France, Canada, Holland, Ireland, England and America. I learnt the French, English and American national anthems. Our headmistress came from Quebec, Canada, but loved great President Dwight Eisenhower of America pointing him out in a history book. He was the first American President I heard of. She said she dated Bing Crosby, a singer and an actor. Each nun enforced their world to us opening up my one track mind. Grandma taught me plenty about Africa and Arabia. Surprisingly,

42

she had visited Europe and heard about the wickedness of Russians and German leaders.

During the Geography lesson, I travelled with a little boy on mother owls back to different parts of the world as a teacher read to us. I felt cold when mother owl and I flew up the freezing Himalaya Mountains. We travelled to the Fujiyama, China, Australia, America and Europe. After every lesson, we tediously practiced hand drawing of maps. Tracing was not allowed. I tried to be as perfect as Atlases were.

Daddy went through our reports with us seated next to him full of anticipation. He appreciated our good work and hugged us when we did particularly well in a subject. Time seemed so short when Daddy had to leave but had made us feel special the little time he spent with us. It was like he had no other children but us.

Back in school we learnt a new language, French. Daddy was excited as he had learnt it in the Congo: a Belgium ruled country. I believe he worked in the Congo at some mine there. He as well spoke Afrikaans from South Africa. I vowed to be as brilliant as Daddy was. I wrote to Daddy with *the* little French I knew, *Bonjour Papa. Comment alley vous? Jai tres bein.* I was so happy learning French. How does one learn another language when not yet perfect in English? My sister Berit was coping with the same predicament as I did. I never asked Daddy why he didn't send me to school in 1954 with my sisters or Berit in 1956 when she was about turning six in March. My life was full of puzzlements.

The good thing about Sister Mary, she let me sit with her as she read Daddy's letter explaining the long words he used. She taught me the use of an Oxford

Dictionary, tested me on spellings of which I'd get all correct.

Our French-Canadian nun, Jijelle, taught us French. She was very good and I got the hang of it easily. Verbs are very complicated. I let Daddy know about my confirmation and that I had joined the Legion of Mary and Brownies. School was so much fun. I asked Daddy if he remembered Berit turned eight on 9th March.

Every holiday, we had great fun with Mummy and Grandma. As usual, I accompanied Grandma uphill, downhill visiting people every day. If she ever decided to visit this rich palace, not far from home, there I was with her. As I admire the piano the King asked me to play a piece. No longer the nervous little child I played *Suku, Suku.* How I wished Daddy was here to hear me play. Daddy had no piano. Anyway, Daddy is overly busy with his new family.

Why don't you take us to your home? I wanted to ask Daddy. Mummy trained us never to question elders; it was *impolite.* I look at Daddy, questioningly, with a tilted head as a puppy does to his master. Anyway, I am very lucky to have a Daddy and a Mummy. I must admit both are loving.

Even though we are in a Muslim home, Mummy, allows us to fetch a Christmas tree up Namirembe Cathedral which we happily decorate. She even stitches new matching dresses for Christmas. Daddy gives us each one hundred shillings pocket money an equivalent to today's dollar. That was a lot of money then! We use it mainly to see children shows at Cinema Halls, buy ice-cream, pay bus fares and do fancy shopping.

I learnt so much about another world called America through watching movies made in Hollywood. We treasured bubble-gum wrappings in scrapbooks.

These taught us about the lives of film stars. Daddy never spoke of movies made in Norway. I don't think Daddy could sit still and watch movies. He'd rather read.

Sylvia was at the top and I tagged along. We were doing a big play for Parents Day. I hoped Daddy would come and see Sylvia act. I never participated in plays not even to recite a poem. I used to write about what went on at school but after a severe warning; I only write about me and my sisters. I had no business telling Daddy about what one child does to another. The nuns warned the older children not to touch younger children. If a student needed discipline; it was to be reported to the Headmistress. I was so happy to hear that. This school was wonderful.

Bjordal Mines Limited,
Nyamolilo,
Uganda,
4th February 1959

Dear daughter,

I am so happy you like your new class and that learning is now much easier and you have a happy friendly teacher. Is your friend alright? During the holidays you said she was very active then she got very ill after she was boxed in the stomach. The nuns should keep an eye on her. They should take her to see a doctor, perhaps she has internal injury. I am glad you are being a mother to her. It is sad they lost their parents when so young. I believe Kenya is now relatively safe. I am afraid the British are not very nice people, not even to the many countries they colonized. I am sure you will learn more about that when you are older.

My love to Helene, Sylvia and Berit,

All the same I thought how my Daddy's hypnotism made me feel better. If he were here, Daddy would have made my friend better. Well, after hospitalization at Princess Margaret Hospital or King George Hospital, she came back just skin and bone.

Alone I sat in the dining room writing to Daddy about sixth grade being the best year of my life. I was not as sickly as I used to be. I measured 5ft 4 inches in height and weighed 105 lbs. Sylvia was much taller and heavier than me. I was chosen in the netball team, as scorer. Sylvia, a terrific runner and defender, grabbed the ball threw it to me and I scored perfectly.

Ninety percent of our time was spent in the classrooms. After silently listening to teachers, we copied page after page of notes from the blackboard. I cracked my head with mathematics. I was grateful to Mummy for introducing multiplications and division when I ran her business at age nine. Daddy encouraged me to expand my imagination in Compositions and Art by pointing out the picturesque mountains, sky, and plants. Both Daddy and Grandma stimulated my interest in History and Geography. I loved Health science because Daddy was literally obsessed with cleanliness, vitamins, treatment of various illnesses, the importance of eating right and being physically active. As for my mind he advised me to read a lot. One thing he never spoke of was religion.

"That is a delicate subject," he'd say. He was liberated like an American.

Recess time is filled with joyous laughter and happy faces; queuing up for a slice of pineapple or a sandwich at ten O'clock. We competed drinking eight glasses per

46

day of rain water from a big tank built in the stages for filtering rain water.

"Drinking pure water is vital for the body and soft drink are like poison to the body." Daddy said.

The nuns had a farm. Helene and many girls did not like farm milk. She said the milk tasted like the cow itself. I once drank the British pasteurized milk at a friend's home; it was yummy. Sometime I sneak to the kitchen and beg for a glass of fresh creamy milk. I did not tell Daddy about this, otherwise he would make the nuns give us milk and I might get into trouble.

Daddy and I love animals. Odd as it may sound I prefer them to people. The reason being that nuns weren't good to cuddly pups and lovely kittens. Sylvia stealthily dragged me to watch something too improbable to imagine. Cute baby animals were put into a sack and drowned in a pool! The very pool where our coffee beans were washed. My big strong Daddy would never do such a thing to animals. Sylvia taught me that God, the creator of animals, said *Thou shalt not kill!* Everything that God created *is good*. So animals are good. I learnt a lot from Sylvia.

Once a year, birds built nests under the top floor roof in preparation for giving birth to eggs. Mummy birds keep the eggs warm until baby birds are hatched. When they grow older they fly off. That is what happened in *our heaven.* Daddy never killed birds.

Sylvia and I watched workers climbing up the ladder, steal the eggs and give them to nuns, *probably to have for breakfast.* Then the men put tar into the birds nest. The poor birds' wings get stuck and they fall to their death; some are partially alive but completely hapless. Soon the whole school gathered and joined us as we cried.

47

Daddy said, *"If you do not like certain persons or animals keep away from them."* Perhaps during the holidays I will tell Daddy to teach the nuns a thing or two. Perhaps he will stop them doing wicked things. *Better watch out. I will get into trouble if I do that.* I knew nothing about misery, or wickedness but love, laughter and respect for nature when I lived with Daddy.

Bjordal Mines Limited,
Kabale,
20th March 1959

My dear Daughter,

A good thing the nuns have taken your friend to hospital. She may have appendicitis. That is probably why she is throwing up. I am sure she will be alright. She may need a small operation. You must be doing your examinations by the time my letter reaches you. I wish you, Helene, Sylvia and Berit best of luck. I am looking forward to seeing you in April.

Remember I told you if you join sports you will get stronger. Good for you Mandy.

Lots of love, Daddy

As I watched over Josephine, in the silent convent; spooky spirits hover around making floors squeak. I feel a dead nun breathing behind my neck. Automatically, I turn toward the back door but see nothing. Another dead nun bangs shut the front door which I had kept wide open in case I needed to take off. The combination of Cardinal floor polish and lilies didn't help either as I associated those two smells with death.

Josephine drifted in and out of sleep begging me to stay with her during the April holidays which around the corner. *My Daddy will be visiting us. My*

48

ticket is already booked," I lamely excused myself, promising to stay with her during August holidays.

"You will not find me here," she said. Death never crossed my mind. I selfishly thought about what I'd do with my time without a soul around? This place is enormous surrounded with huge coffee farms, an orchard, a huge school building, vast compounds, villages and a cemetery. Moreover, my drugged friend slept most of the time. There was no radio. I was not allowed to bring a story book just in case it was contaminated. As soon as I start telling Josephine made up stories, of which she insist of me, she falls asleep. Maybe she is listening. I sing to her whilst stroking her forehead. I am the only human by her bedside. Had I known she was to die when I was away; I would have sacrificed my holidays.

I was so happy to see Daddy the first week of our arrival from Kenya. *He asked us how we felt health-wise. Was the school good to us? Were we happy? Did we have enough to eat?* Going through our reports, he asked us why we did not do so well in such and such subject. Meanwhile Mummy brought tea accompanied with biscuits. I silently thought how suspended I was between two individual parents. This continuous thought never left my mind. I never accepted my parents' separation. They never fought or screamed at each other nor did we witness big angry dramas or arguments. Now Daddy is like a guest. This is his house. He built it. I wanted to show him our big bedroom. When Daddy visited us at Kisubi, again he was as a stranger. The nun sat *between* us directly opposite Daddy guarding us like we were prisoners. Helene had made me vow to tell Daddy what was done to us. I swore I would only if Daddy takes us on a

49

picnic at Entebbe's Botanical Gardens or at Lake Victoria Hotel far away from the school. He did not so we sat docile and answered questions asked. We sadly waved goodbye at his white Chevrolet going down the dusty path covered in a cloud of red dust.

I told Daddy we were the only Norwegian in the whole of East Africa and the school. Very few girls had Goan or South Indian Catholic fathers. Indian tribes kept to their caste, religion and schools in Nairobi. The British didn't mind Indians doing that. After all they imported their grandfathers to build the Kenyan railway line to begin with.

I wrote to Daddy how happy I was seeing him during April holidays. We missed the train and as usual chased it from Kampala to Jinja in a taxi. How exciting that was for us but not for Mummy. Some holidays we missed it even at Jinja and disappointedly missed a few days of school. One time, the nuns came late to pick us up at Nairobi Station. As we were left isolated uncertain of being picked and it was getting dark Helene suggested we go to Great Grandma at Shauri Moyo. We spent two weeks. I was very uncomfortable and quietly asked Great Grandma to take us back to school. She paid a tenant, Mr. Kamau, a total stranger, to take us thirty seven miles to Mangu.

> *Bjordal Mines Limited,*
> *Kabale,*
> *30th May 1959*

My dear daughter,

I had a letter from the nuns that you missed the train and that you did not return to school for two weeks! I have been away otherwise I would have found out what happened to you from your mother.

50

They say you were brought to school in a taxi! That you had stayed in Shauri Moyo with your Great grandma. Why do that? The nuns came late, for God sakes, to pick you and did not find you. You are very irresponsible. Anything could have happened to you and your Mother, the school or I would not have known. Please tell the other girls never to do that again. You have to wait at the station for the school to pick you or ask the police for help.

This has made me very concern and very upset.

Your loving,

Daddy

Whatever my Daddy said was correct. Travelling to Kenya was not a short trip, mind you. Everything in this colonial country is different from our Monarch ruled country, Uganda. If by any chance we got lost in Uganda we would mention Grandma's name and would be automatically escorted back home. Practically the whole of Namirembe knew our Grandma and Mother.

I profoundly apologized for causing Daddy concern in a letter. I could not complain enough when the cold season starts. The nuns dressed us in vests under our petticoats then a blouse and finally a sweater; I still felt terribly cold and often got asthma.

I struggled juggling with fourteen subjects in all. The difficult ones were done from eight to twelve o'clock: art and craft, singing, literature, drama and sports in the afternoons. I told Daddy everything; going for confession every week, mass every day and retreats for a week, once a term. Not a sound came from our throats only writing notes was allowed. We read books of saints, the Bible, and meditations and prayed the rosary in church and had lectures from visiting priests. I told Daddy I daily prayed for him.

51

Daddy and I kept in touch the whole of 1959. To cheer Daddy up, I told him about the great fun I had in the Girl Guides club, the Legion of Mary with organized outings.

During Lent we were privileged to watch plenty of Biblical movies with Charlton Heston. Due to my height, I was put at the back row therefore straining my eyes to watch a blurry movie called *The Robe*. The Jews were terrible to this man Jesus. My sufferings were nowhere near comparison to what He went through. I decided never again to complain about my pains just bear them.

I was terrified when our healthy Head-girl died of pneumonia. I was so grateful I only had asthma. That would not kill me.

My way of thinking completely changed in this school. Naughtiness amongst the children was quite permissible. *It was fun being up to no good as long as you weren't caught.* Girls would do anything to be sent out of the class practically every day of the week. Handsome boys drove teachers up the walls. Sister Mary De Lorette was called to straighten us out when a teacher couldn't. I often gathered little unhappy-looking children, in circles and told them adventurous stories of Daddy. We played games their laughter echoed like at the mine when I was up in *heaven* with my Daddy.

Meanwhile, I watched Sylvia farther down the compound aiming at the goal post. Sometime she did hockey or hop scotch. She never seemed to hear the bell or see the whole school running and lining in front of their classes but continued playing.

End of the year is an important time. We did final examination papers using a nip pen; every so often

52

dipping the nip into a bottle of blue Quick Ink: carefully blotting so no word is smudged.

It's unbelievable I have completed five years of primary school. I'm so excited to go to secondary school something rare for women in 1960.

The Queen and the Duke of Edinburgh are scheduled to visit Kenya. Lucky me, a privilege Girl Guide, was among throngs of people in Nairobi waving the British flag as I did in 1954, up Namirembe Hill, Uganda. I had hoped to find my lost Daddy amongst hundreds of dignitaries following a procession of cars. But he was not there. I gathered he must be overly busy with his new family.

Nyamolilo Wolfram,
Kabale, Uganda,
14th November 1960

My dear daughter,

Didn't I tell you? I am so proud Mandy you have joined all these clubs for your betterment. Now I want you to really study for your finals. That will determine whether or not you can go to secondary school. If you do, you will make my day. I do not want you to give up school and do commercial classes as most girls are doing and land working in offices. It is not bad but what is important is completing school and perhaps getting into a college. However, concentrate on this first then we will see what happens in the future.

I wish you all the best,
Daddy

Daddy's visits made all the difference my entire life. Although he had that body-builder appearance; he was as gentle as a lamb. I had wanted to ask him for books to read during the holidays as we had none at

53

home, but I did not. Imported novels were a rare commodity. I remember a Goan girl handing us a heavy suitcase to carry to her brother, a teacher in Kampala. On one trip Sylvia came up with an idea.

"What if I find out what is in this suitcase that we are given to carry every holiday?" So she worked on it and voila she unlocked it! Lo and behold in there were stamped **White Sisters** library books! We had no idea how many books this girl stole from the school. We were accomplices! We would have been humiliated in front of the whole school maybe expelled! The next holiday we refused her suit-case.

When we got our usual pocket money; movies were first on our agenda. What a treat that was. Every Saturday evenings we dressed up and went to early shows. Movies were strictly censored at this time. Nineteen-sixty-two was another great year for me. I was elected a class prefect and was crowned the most popular girl in the secondary school. Not that I was beautiful, outstanding in sports, drama or music. The crown should have been given to Sylvia. My poor sister Berit was so teased by the older girls calling her, *Nyonyo*. That's what she said to anyone who teased her; *nyonyo, nyonyo.* Her, *heathen,* Norwegian name Berit was replaced by Elizabeth after Jesus' aunt, definitely, not after Queen Elizabeth II. Unfortunately, I did not pamper my sisters as Helene used to. I hoped they would independently take care of themselves. As soon as we arrived home, Mummy informed us that Daddy was admitted into Mulago Hospital. Without unpacking, we took a bus to Kampala then another to Mulago. We crept stealthily into the room just in case he was asleep. Daddy's face lit up giving us a lovely, warm smile. We bent over and kissed him. He said he

54

was bored doing nothing in hospital. He handed us the key and said to wait for him in the car. Which sick father in a hospital would feel obligated to drop their children home? Daddy was unbelievably protective. Mummy was shocked to see us sooner than expected. Alone with Daddy at the sitting room, we conspired to go dancing at a teenage dance up Mayembe hill not too far from home. In the evening he came in a well pressed suit looking even more handsome. We made sure not to wear makeup. Daddy hated makeup to the core. How happy and proud the three of us were dancing with Daddy. How tired he must have been but never happier dancing away with three daughters. Our friends teased us that our fifty-year old Daddy was our boyfriend. That was another day I'll never forget.

Maryhill School 1954-1964

CHAPTER FOUR
FINALLY WITH DADDY

As the smoky train chugged in and out hills and valleys, up and down mountains in the White Highlands, Kenya, Sylvia, Berit and I were excited to go home to Uganda after three months! Without a moments' doubt I know my Daddy will visit us at the normal hour, the normal day in *our* sitting room. This time *we* shall be honoured to serve him tea and ginger biscuits on a tray covered with Mummy's crotched cloth.

Mummy announced the greatest surprise of my life! She gently said, *"Your father is taking you to the mine."* I could have screamed my throat sore and touched the sky but that's not how mature people behave. Ulfhild and the boys left for Norway; Daddy had told Mummy. He was finally free to take us on a holiday to my *heaven*. Because we lived almost over seven thousand feet above sea level, way high up above clouds; I had believed it was *heaven.*

All I could remember of beautiful Ulfhild was her unfriendly attitude towards me when I was little. I, however, never dwelt on that subject. Every time Daddy visited us, I begged him to take me back so I could see my brothers.

"I'm so sorry Mandy. Ulfhild does not want to involve you with the boys. One thing I want you to know is that I shall always love you," he'd say.

Daddy had always been too self-analytical to pretend to be anything else. I understood him and accepted Daddy's apology.

I was born during severe discrimination in East Africa. What Ulfhild did was acceptable then. She was

56

protecting her sons just in case something drastic happened to them whilst playing with us. This was how my brain reasoned. Aunt Liv and Uncle Sverre did not keep us at arm's length with their daughter. An African or a coloured child was treated like someone with a plague, except the Missionaries. The Catholic religion taught me to, *Love our enemies, do good to those that hate you* and a whole list of them. Therefore Ulfhild and my half-brothers are not enemies. Anyone who had Daddy's blood was good as far as I was concerned. Daddy sons are *my* brothers like it or not.

When Sylvia died of cancer in 1981, I wrote to Ulfhild asking her to give the dismay news to our brothers. She wrote back an unbelievably harsh letter refraining me from ever getting in touch with her or my brothers. *"As it is they already have gone through enough trauma their lives through."* A good thing, we, Daddy's thick-skinned African children, were never traumatized. Heaven helps me! Wasn't I traumatized my entire life? I vowed never to marry an ex-married man with children. A single, Catholic man was my only option. Mother was not sure of the date Daddy was coming. All the same we packed. She said Daddy was to buy us coats and Mackintosh boots as it is extremely cold up at Kigezi.

"Do we really need winter outfits in Africa with the Equator passing right through Uganda?" we doubtfully asked Mummy.

"You will be surprised how cold it is at Kigezi. You can touch the clouds up there," she assured us. What a pity, Helene was at Preston, England, continuing with nursing.

I hardly slept that night. Next morning I watched the main road for Daddy as I did in nineteen forty-nine,

57

at four years old. Elegant women dressed in *Busuti* passed by with heavy basket well balanced on top of their heads. They asked me what I was doing alone by the roadside.

"Don't you know? I'm waiting for my Daddy. Have you seen him? He has a dimple on his chin and a gold side tooth and eyes like the sky." The silly women walked off giggling . I had hoped Daddy would visit me at *my* new home at Nankulyabe. My constant questions *When is my Daddy coming home?:* irritated Mummy so much that she sent me to a nearby African Nursery school. Children gathered around me. Again I was laughed at. One little boy threw a stone at me and I was carried home screaming my head off, blood trailing down my forehead to my eye and down the left cheek.

"I want my Daddy. I didn't tell you to send me to horrible children," I screamed at Mummy tears flowing down my redden hot face. Mummy cleaned me up and put me in visiting Grandma's arms. I vaguely heard Mummy say I was upset because my father had new woman, a dancer, from a Mombasa club. Grandma scolded Mummy for publicizing family secrets.

"Not to worry my little one, I will teach you to dance like an Arab," Grandma squeezed me. Perhaps if I knew how to dance like this new mummy, Daddy might take me back. I seriously learnt Arabic dancing from Grandma.

Mummy put the fear of hell about kidnapping, even though it was non-existent in Africa then. However, being stubborn there I was back to the road. A young girl was kept at a distant to keep an eye on me.

Now at eighteen, I unbelievably watched the road from the window! One's personality never really changes.

58

We gave up waiting for Daddy and travelled by car to Kabale, a unique clean little town. It had a White Horse hotel, a bank, a Bus Park, all sorts of shops run by Indians, offices run by Europeans and a small hospital and a Post Office. *That's where my letters arrived.* We slept at a hotel exhausted beyond reason. The piercing night cold is something I shall never forget. Low dark clouds collided with each other and thunder echoed from nearby mountains. Kabale is infinitely cooler than any part of Uganda. No wonder Mummy said we needed coats and Wellington boots. We woke up in a grey misty town covered in clouds. I gulped a scalding cup of tea, burning my tongue. After making enquiries about the *Bjordal Mines*, we ventured to the unknown. The driver had almost given up when I shouted 'There, there it is the *Bjordal Mine sign.'* He screeched, reversed and turned into a mud path. I had expected him to automatically know *my* important Daddy. His name was on Road Maps.

We drove some thirty odd miles engulfed in thick cold clouds. Goddesses kept clearing the way for us. Soon the mountains, burnished with red-gold, appeared as we sailed above creamy-pink clouds, liken to strawberry ice-cream. Driving higher and higher was like a slow flight in an aeroplane. Down and down we descended to the mine. The man, precipitated on crossing the reed-bound bridge with five of us in the car!

"Are you crazy or what?" I daringly warned him about quicksand beneath the dark, green still water. Daddy had warned me of that when I was little. Mummy severely said wicked gods silently wait there and swallow stupid people crossing that bridge.

59

Springing out of the car I crossed this unsteady, floating bridge on foot followed by my sisters, Sylvia and Berit, our luggage in hand. Balancing with arms holding on to the ropes; we startled a colourful long tailed bird and it flew off in haste, its flustering wings quite audible. Miners sprang to life from nowhere and surrounded us jostling and jabbering and scanning us. They knew Ulfhild, Haakon and Braaken but not us. Up the unnerving dusty road we clambered, seven thousand feet, like early explorers as cold sweat tingled down our spines. By half way, we were quite parched and exhausted. The breathe of wind blew dried leaves rustling passed us. Withered flowers splayed dust of pollen onto our faces making Sylvia sneeze. She had terrible allergy. For the fun of it, we made nonsensical noises then listened to echoes reverberate in the valley below. Thick, sinister mist cooled us as we struggled uphill.

After almost an hour, we finally reached the top of this majestic house, *my castle in heaven*, liken a crown upon a mountain. Even though Mserekano and Barnado conveyed extraordinary joy: welcoming us indoors, I stood there at the verandah mesmerized with the surrounding beauty below. There I was chasing Helene and cousin Svanhild. Differences in language or colour did not matter. Svanhild spoke Norsk and a little Kiswahili whilst we spoke almost three African languages. I was utterly disappointed when the servant and cook said Daddy had just left for Kampala this very day! I had wanted to save him the six hundred miles trip back and forth. Not that I thought he was ill or anything but he had turned forty-eight years old this June. That is old, so I thought. The well-trained servants carried hot water in the bath then served us delicious mutton stew: reliving my childhood for a minute.

Six o'clock in the morning tea with Carnation creamy milk was brought to our bed! I had never been served morning tea in bed in my life! This is wonderful, I smiled wishing Helene was here too.

I sneaked into Daddy's tidy bedroom. The drawers, cupboards, everything was spic-span. My Daddy is the most orderly man in the world. His office and storeroom were just as neat. Perhaps discipline was ingrained in him whilst in the navy as a sailor at just seventeen. In my mind of minds, I believed men in general were meticulous, particular and precise. I was to later learn that is quite the contrary; neatness is not a male thing. *Why do women make such a big thing about trivial things like washing of hands and tidiness?* That's what I heard and still hear men say. In his lounge were low shelves with orderly arranged magazine and books: the Evening Post, British Telegraph, the Independent, Time Magazines, Financial Times, the Britannia and Geographical Magazines. *Books, wonderful books.*

After two days, entirely on our own, rising echoes of a car amplified to the top of the mountain. Excitedly we rushed to the verandah. How happy Daddy was beaming with joy. He embraced and hugged us. He did not scold us for making a waste trip to Kampala and back. Barnado and Mserekano helped with boxes and boxes of food and accordingly arranged them in the big neat store I had inspected earlier on. Even though I had good training not to go prying into other people's privacy; I should have known better. What I did was a sin that needed confession. For heaven sakes, this is *my* Daddy home!

61

Daddy was a driven business man and a stern disciplinarian. He left for work before we had risen. After an early breakfast we were on the verandah watching a few blue haze of smoke twirling in the air from the opposite lower mountains. People lived there even though we never saw anyone. I told my sisters how I could differentiate smells of goats, cows, chicken and smoke when I was little.

The year nineteen sixty-three, I felt truly re-kindled and bonded with Daddy making up for time lost. It was almost as if nothing ever happened between us. My memory of my *heaven* was irreplaceable. I've written everything there in my first book, Where Do We Belong? How proud of me Daddy would have been had he read my book. He so often said, *"As for you Mandy I can see you become a writer."*

Daddy was still as handsome as he was when I was little with a Kirk Douglas' deep cleft in his chin, a Pat Boone smile, and Charlton Heston's or Sean Connery's body built. In the evenings, together, we watched the vast scenes of mountains covered with greenery and flowers plummeting down valleys below. A distant moon washed the lush landscape glittering the peaks. How many years had I missed *my heaven,* a world of silence serene filled with soft music of crickets, frogs and an occasional hoot from a hidden owl up some darkened tree. How can anyone fall asleep when in *heaven*? I was unafraid of night shadows when a moving cloud passed beneath this huge bulb. I breathed in fresh air. Mind you, the cold up here could easily freeze your nose. But, I did not want to miss those moments of bliss. You never know, I may never have this opportunity again.

As we sat in the lounge enjoying a cup of Ovaltine Daddy backed up his adventures with an album and loose photographs. What a lively happy life he had; skiing in the air, good at all sorts of sports. He travelled a lot. Every time I heard the song of Ricky Nelson, *I'm a Travelling Man,* meeting beautiful women, made me think that's how my Daddy was a young handsome sailor, among hundreds of sailors, naval officers and a contingent of marine. He was a pilot too and was contemplating on buying a helicopter. He showed us an old South African newspaper carefully folded and kept in the album with a write up of him on the Limpopo rough River at twenty seven years. There was an article in the Norwegian newspaper about Daddy's mine. He later made a trip across the Sahara in a white car and he wrote two chronicle articles about it in some magazine. Louis Leaky visited him and they explored areas for pre-historic bones.

Next day, I was overwhelmed seeing the inside of the mine just one more time, inching and slithering in tunnels, just a little. We stooped our heads watchfully, dropping on hands and knees as the cavern narrowed. I felt cold in the shafts due to dampness. An abundance of mosses and ferns healthily blossomed. When fear-sweat broke, Daddy cautioned us not go in any further. Outside Daddy encouraged us to hold a powerful water-pipe that jetted water strong enough to break off rocks. We dare not put our hand over the water as our whole arm would be dislocated, *"This is powerfully evocative,"* Daddy said.

Come evening, Daddy taught us ballroom dances the Waltz, the Foxtrot, Viennese Waltzed and

63

Quickstep as he played His Master's Voice long LPs. That is when I developed an appreciation of Johann Strauss, Tchaikovsky, Dvorak Antonin and Frederic Chopin music rather than wild pop music.

Daddy loved his mountain with a passion as he did the African weather. I guess Kabale was cool enough for Europeans. He talked of great English men who helped open big cotton and coffee businesses upraising Uganda's economy as early as 1903-1909. Wow, Grandma was a little girl then living with the Sultan of Zanzibar. Well, Daddy had trained me to record everything in my brain. Great white men organized Uganda. D. Lawrence, M. Chenery, Frederick Crawford even Lady Baden Power visited Uganda in 1930. She and her husband started Girl Guides and Boy Scout, respectively. The Toro Mills sent Toro flour to Belgium from 1914-1918 during World War I. Twenty thousand Ugandan men joined the army in World War II.

I was so disappointed missing Christmas with Daddy in 1963. I reluctantly accompanied Mummy to Zanzibar. My sisters chose Daddy over Mummy. Daddy always encouraged me to take every opportunity in life for my betterment even as a sacrifice so I went on this unknown trip. *"Whatever the circumstances there is something new to learn and broaden your mind."* Daddy always said to me. I gave Daddy an outline of my trip.

What an adventure I had. First of all, the ship to Zanzibar was packed beyond capacity. Stubborn Mummy insisted we board it anyway even if we had to stand. We were directed below the deck. What a shock hit me in the face, when I saw hundreds of people horded like slaves of hundreds of years ago. Except these people were well dressed, their skin a natural

64

matte texture, their flawless faces gleaming with sweat. The captain diplomatically explained to Mummy that was the only option we had. On seeing the crowd Mummy gave every possible excuse how sickly I was. Watching the constant sea spray against the ship, stifling and reeking of oil, the motion of hazy water made me feel unwell and my colour turned white.

As the sailors furl the sails, my nose began to bleed. The captain realized I was genuinely sick. Laying me down on a bunk in his cabin, he placed a cold compression on my head. Before you could say Jack Robinson, I retched all over his neat clean outfit and all over the cabin. Nothing could stop me until I had no bouts of bile left. He unbelievably cleaned the cabin floor whilst Mummy, *the princess,* watched. The voyage was a nightmare. Next morning I was fit as a fiddle.

The men in Zanzibar appeared serious looking, unlike my smiling Daddy. How I wished he were here to experience this different world. Every woman including tourists dressed modestly, blending in with the crowd all over the town, beaches, and sidewalks. How romantic it was watching the harbour lights and quiet sea lapping at the rocks. Waves pounding at beaches washed birds, combing the beach in search of any morsel of food swept ashore. Murmuring waves always lulled me to sleep in steaming hot nights.

Dressed like an Arab woman, I attentively listened to mysterious Arabic and beautiful musical Kiswahili. I kicked myself for not taking the opportunity to learn it for Grandma. I loved everything about Zanzibar: the Arabic dances, the spicy tantalizing food; the huge ocean and the beach covered with big shells. Daddy would have loved the fish curries and big yellow-red mangoes.

On Zanzibar's Independence Day, we were privileged to have front seats at the stadium directly opposite the Duke of Edinburgh and the Sultan.

Entertaining my thoughts I daydreamed Daddy in a white *kanzu* and a *Fez* looking like Peter O'Toole in Lawrence of Arabia and me, like actress Sally Field in *Not Without My Daughter*, movie dragging me to meet the Duke and the Sultan. I even saw us arrested by Zanzibari official for obstructions. I came back to reality when band parades marched across the stadium. I listened to the tall, handsome Duke and the Sultan speak. I was disappointed not to have met my Arab Grandfather although I did, however, meet his skinny second wife and family.

In the last week of our holidays, we visited royalties; friends of Grandma, at the opulent palace. I thanked Daddy for encouraging me to see the side of the coin.

Bjordal Mine Limited,
Kabale,
30th December 1963.

My dear Mandy,

I am so glad you are enjoying yourself. I'm sending this letter to Mombasa as you say you will be there on Christmas day. You also say Romeo is taking you dancing and Mother has agreed. The girls are here with me at the mine. We plan a lovely Christmas. I am so happy you saw the Duke so close. You should have gone across the stadium and shook hands with him. Did you find an Arab prince to whisk you away? You would become a Muslim, you know. I am just joking.

I am so sorry you got travel sickness. That's a problem I noticed you have. When you travel by ship you breathe in salty air that dries your throat. You should have drunk plenty of water. The nose bleeding you inherited that from me, unfortunately. You must have looked pretty in Arabic outfits.

Well, I will not say much as I do not know when you will get my letter before you return. I wish you a Merry Christmas and have fun with Romeo.

Lots of love and have fun,
Daddy

Back to Uganda, after a terrible bus journey in flooded Kenya, I immediately got in touch with Daddy. I was sure glad to see him and my sisters; talking non-stop about the wonderful Island of spices, Zanzibar. Spices were introduced to Africa by the English, Europeans, Arabs, Chinese and Indians. Zanzibar is absolutely romantic. I took Daddy's sound advice on the importance of education very seriously so I allowed no *charming Arabian prince to carry me away.* Daddy made it clear that education and self-sufficiency were of greater value than a rushed marriage. If not of Daddy assuring love and encouragement, I would never have taken my education seriously. I was loaded with a list of excuses not to cope with school work: sent to school late, discriminations, constant illness, and the negative opinion about not educating girls.

As Daddy watched me sitting at the verandah, he was amazed I had so many of his little habits like the leaking of my lips and the shaking of a leg when concentrating. He said, *"Normally children acquire habitual habits from parents when they live with them. You have not grown up with me yet and you amazingly do exactly as I do!"*

67

I had browsed through a book called *The Sacred and the Profane* about the nature of religion by Mircea Eliade written in fifties from Daddy's library. Though it was interesting, I put it down knowing too well I would have to go for confession reading such a book. My Daddy would read any book he could lay his hands on early civilizations, peoples of the world and religions. How could fate have robbed me of reading for nine years! *"Don't worry Mandy,"* Daddy said giving me examples of famous disadvantaged people of wars even the blind children falsely put into retarded institutions because they were short-sighted and could not read. All that was needed was *prescription glasses.* Many became Authors! Maybe one day, I will write a book in English.

My Daddy in his habitat

Mummy's Girls

Exciting honeymoon in jungle

A HONEYMOON trip by car through 1,000 miles of East African jungle to her new home on a wolfram mine in Uganda was one of the most exciting but nerve-shattering experiences of her life, said Mrs. Harald Bjordal, who is on a visit to her parents, Mr. and Mrs. L. N. Short, of Wayville West.

Nor is it the least romantic part of her story. Nine months ago, Mrs. Bjordal, then Margaret Short, left in the cargo ship Pemba for a holiday with relatives in Mombasa, East Africa. While there she met and married her Norwegian husband, who is owner of the largest wolfram mine in East Africa, and is also owner of a goldmine.

They were married in the Anglican cathedral in Mombasa early in January, with Kay Little, of Perth, a fellow passenger in the Pemba, as bridesmaid. After two weeks' honeymoon in Mombasa they set out by car for the mine.

The baby son of Mr. and Mrs. Harald Bjordal, of Kabale, Uganda, British East Africa, will be christened Reynold David, in St. Augustine's Church, Unley. Godparents will be Mrs. Peter Milton (baby's aunt), Miss Betty Stone, and Messrs. Ian Kennett, L. R. Short and David Short.

While in Adelaide, Mrs. Bjordal is staying with her parents, Mr. and Mrs. L. N. Short, at Wairoa, Wayville.

1950

71

CHAPTER FIVE
OVER WITH SCHOOLING

Bjordal Mines Limited
Director: Harald Bjordal
Kabale.
15ᵗʰ January 1964

My dearest Daughter,
You say that all sorts of professionals and religious people came to talk you about careers; mainly teaching, nursing, secretary, including a Catholic mother who has had five daughters in five years! That is quite a career. So the nuns did not approve of you and Sylvia being airhostesses? What right do they have? They claimed these jobs were not on the agenda and moreover not decent jobs? What the heck?
I'm sorry you had to choose being a teacher and Sylvia a nurse there and then. But every experience in this world upgrades you. Get as many certificates as you possibly can. I was a sailor. I delivered newspaper and I played the accordion to earn pocket money. I did anything. Helene will complete her two years nurses' course in England this year. Next year, the three of you will face the world. I wish you all the luck!
                              Your loving father,
                              Daddy

Daddy gave me an excellent example of what a man ought to be: disciplined, straightforward, loving, hardworking, honest, responsible and family committed. It's beyond me when I hear strong men beating up their wives or their own flesh and blood.

With the world today, my concept of some men has unfortunately changed.

Of course, Daddy knew it all but he did not want to dishearten me what life was really all about. Daddy said experience in the world was beneficial. *It backs and toughens you up.* I thought about that my entire life. Whenever I could not solve a situation I reread Daddy's letters and got the answer I needed.

It angered me so much that the nuns had to read my letters to and from Daddy. I decided to write one through the nuns and one through my Indian day scholars begging him not mention anything out of the ordinary. I wrote that Sylvia and I planned to become Air-hostesses, a chance to see the world. Well, the principal randomly said, "Margaret you are going to Highridge Teachers Training College in January 1965. As for you, Sylvia, you are to train as a nurse at Nairobi Hospital starting in September 1965." I wanted to scream that *my Daddy said I could become a writer or a poet or an artist,* but I was dumb-founded. A teacher? What a boring, low-paid job was that!

Daddy was proud I was elected the schools' Head Girl. What a privilege that was and what a responsibility. I wasn't thrilled but was rather petrified. If you are not popular with the girls they could give you hell. Nothing like physical bullying existed, it was mostly verbal. We really lived like one loving family, when I think of it.

I spoke to Sister Aristide, a wonderful saintly nun, begging her to intervene for me. She held my hand and gently said it was God's plan and that I should accept it. God would guide me, and was certain I would be a wonderful Head Girl. What frightened me most was Sylvia, a true comedian. She had all sorts of funny

73

excuses making the girls laugh when I reprimanded her for being late. She then hugged and kissed me.

I struggled with three English papers: grammar, literature and composition. The sciences are in four parts: physics, biology, health science and chemistry, with mathematics: geometry, algebra and arithmetic. Geography had the physical and contours which I hated to the core. I loved History but had to give it up to continue with French now taught by our Headmistress, Sister Anastasia, with an annoying English accent. After one term, I gave up French. Sylvia continued with it.

I wonder what Daddy would have done had I studied in Uganda? Would he have re-organized the time table to help me do the subjects I loved instead of the way subjects were grouped? I would not have minded a half hour of French and a half hour of History. Daddy would have paid for extra tuition as he did when I was younger. Anyway, I borrowed and read History books from my friends. *"Are you crazy or what to be interested in English and European History?"* they asked. *"What with cramming dates and important dead persons."*

I was so proud of Daddy's bold printed letters **Bjordal Mines Limited,** right across palm-size aerogrammes, *Par Avion,* air letters. At the right corner was the director as (Norwegian).

> *Nyamolilo Wolfram,*
> *Kabale,*
> *Uganda,*
> *10th February 1964.*

My dear Mandy,

I am so proud you have been elected as Head Girl. That proves you are intelligent and responsible. Perhaps you have the wisdom of keeping your temper at bay with your peers. Anyway, I have never known you being aggressive. I am sure the girls will love you and not give unnecessary concern.

About the subjects, do not worry. The more the better, even if you do not sit for them. I am sorry to hear your French teacher has left. She had done a good job with both of you. Well, you can learn all the history you want to know from me. I have hundreds of books here. Do you want me to have a talk with Sylvia? Yes, I did laugh a lot. She is a great happy child as far as I am concern.

I do not have much news at the moment. I'm always as busy as ever. Time has gone so fast. I cannot believe my girls are now teenagers and maturing. And what progress you have made over the years! I knew you could do it.

With the fondest love,
Daddy

I began contemplating that Sister Anastasia did not like mix bred children. Over the nine years, I was at Maryhill the French, American-Canadians, and Dutch nuns were wonderful to us.

Daddy had prepared me for discriminations. A dark-head Austrian- German called Hitler turned Europe into hell on earth. Jews were not only from Palestine, Jerusalem and Israel as Grandma had told me but all over Europe. Daddy didn't know what he was talking about as did my very experienced Grandma, I thought. What about how females were treated?

75

Many thirteen year olds or a little older girls were put into commercial classes or into nursing after seventh grade instead of continuing secondary school. Years later, Daddy told me the whole world did that to women. Some English fathers sent their children to England for further education. Daddy's dream was to send us to Switzerland when very young. Under the new English Headmistress' administration, the slightest provocation from any girl triggered the nun to throw them out of school. That began with one of Sylvia's outspoken friend. Fortunately, another congregation of nuns in Nairobi accepted her. She was top of the class. No longer able to tolerate the music teacher, I too gave up music. I dare not tell Daddy the real reason; as he would definitely have fought back.

Sylvia, Elvira and I were the only half castes privileged to sit for the Cambridge School Certificate. The rest were Goans, Seychellois and a few Indian Day Scholars. After Independence, we had plenty of African girls in Form One, the first class of secondary school; our dear Canadian nun, Sister Aristide, taught Church History. That class put Sylvia to sleep. She actually loudly snored and made the class giggle. We loved our amazing Canadian Art teacher, a nun called Gaitan. She took us outdoors to paint scenes. That's what Daddy hoped I'd do when he pointed at the sky and nature when I was little. I had hoped to take one of my paintings to Daddy but it was only a hopeful dream.

Once and only once, was there an altercation amongst the half-caste and Seychellois girls. So I watched this rowdy gathering from a distance. Sylvia would not miss it for the world. The strangest thing was that the Seychellois girls were more or less like the half castes only that they were more French, Chinese or

76

African blood from Mozambique. They had been ruled by the French, therefore, had French names and they spoke Creole. Their home was the Seychelles Islands.

Nyamolilo Wolfram,
Kabale,
22nd February 1964,

My dear daughter,

Thanks for your informative letter. I got a letter at the same time from Sister Anastasia concerning Sylvia and Berit. I have written to her and have given her a piece of my mind which I am not going into detail at this precise moment. We shall talk about it when you come home in April. Be strong and persevere the trials you face. Remember I said whatever happens to you in life is a learning phase. Use it as an opportunity.

Yes, I did laugh about Sylvia. Typical her, isn't it? But be firm with her anyway. She will play you up and might get you into trouble. My younger brother, Sverre, was the same. Hope the girls are doing well and keeping well out of mischief. Helene is doing fine in Preston, England. She should finish a little before you and Sylvia do. I do not want you to rush into marriage as your school mates have done. What a loss of youth and a fun time that would be.

Well, my dear, do take care of Sylvia and my baby Berit.

Love,
Daddy

Sometime, I wished Daddy was not as open, honest, and outspoken as he was. His letters got me into serious trouble and I was called to the office. I was instructed to read what Daddy had *dared* write to a nun. I was asked what I thought of my Daddy. I finally spoke up, "I *think we should pray for my Daddy.*" The nun seriously stared right through me.

I quickly sent a letter through a day pupil telling him what happened and advising him never to call a holy woman names like a *frustrated b* .... Daddy was livered when his ten and twelve year old daughters were called street girls for innocently taking photographs in swimsuits. *She could at least call them twerps or little scamps.* Hard as she tried to get me to side with her; Daddy was my hero.

I appreciated Daddy standing up for us. I should have warned him beforehand that no one messes with this English nun. I can't say I was proud with what Daddy wrote but was humiliated. He had no idea that nuns are God's chosen people. Even Kenya's ministers are called to the office if their children make trouble.

To cheer Daddy up I wrote that for the first time we went dancing at the Mangu Boys High School. I was responsible for the girls. Of course, dear sister Alfred kept an eye on us. "*When you are picked for a dance, make sure you keep an arm's distance,*" we were instructed. We literally fought to keep at arm's length when slow music was played. I had an amusing love letter from my partner brought to school by a worker. *You look like a star and the moon* and what have you. What was the boy thinking? He could have got me expelled! Tearing up the letter into shreds, I flushed it down the new flush toilets. No more pit latrines with the ammonia hitting my sinuses and making me feel like throwing up. The Primary School still used those. It was a training process.

Daddy and I believed in justice if it ever existed. Although, he was a young father; he took that

78

responsibility very seriously. Even though we did not have both parents in our daily life; they individually did a good job with us. I have no words to describe how much I learnt from these two individuals.

Nyamolilo Wolfram,
Kabale,
9th March 1964.

My dearest Daughter Mandy,

First of all, I wish Berit a very happy birthday. Today is her fourteenth birthday. I am glad to hear that everything is fine with you, Sylvia and Berit. Now listen to me girls, please keep to the school rules. You can wear swimsuits here at the mine to your hearts' content. I have a camera and so do you Mandy. You can take all the photographs that you want.

At the moment, the three of you have important examinations coming up. Concentrate on that. If you are bored on Sundays, play some sports or read an adventurous book. I understand what it is to be a teenager. There's never enough to do and one does not want to lose a moment of fun. Life is very trying for teenagers. I wish the nuns and teachers understood that. Luckily for me, in Europe, we had newspaper delivering and I earned a little pocket money. We had parks to go to for the day, we swam, and we skied. Of course, winter sickens me to this very day. I hate the European weather.

Well, my dears, wishing you the best of luck. Soon all will be over.

Love,
Daddy

I never thought being a teenager was a problem. Those were the best times of my life. Mummy who was a teenage mother enforced early maturity upon us. It never worked. We danced and sang *foreign* Pop songs and watched uncensored three O'clock American movies. With the rather young nuns, oh boy, we were cultured to be ladylike almost like royalties: your deportment, conduct, posture, aptitude, how you sat, how you stood, your tone of voice. In other Catholic schools, curtsy was on the agenda. At Maryhill, we lowered our eyes when talking to nuns.

Girls from Kenya were luckier than us from other countries like Uganda or Tanzania. Every Sunday, their parents visited and took them on picnics. When I first went to Maryhill, I watched friends from a distant looking forlorn and perhaps a pitiable sight. My friends' parents had no choice but to take me along. I felt loved and a sense of belonging with these wonderful families. I, for one, missed Daddy terribly. In a way, it angered me when Mummy said it was her choice to leave him. She preferred civilization and celebrating with the royal family. What guided me most my entire school life were my Daddy's letters.

Daddy was happy to hear that church attendance was now optional. I still attended mass every day as it had become a vital part of my life even though the girls teased me for being saintly. Out of two hundred children, sometime only five turned up for mass. I remembered how first graders to fourth formers ages 6 to 17 marched to church on a daily bases. You can understand why it was in my system and also the very reason why many girls hated going to church. Severe restrictions in religion can turn one against the church as it did to my Daddy.

Our American teacher, Miss Malloy, finally left end of the term after teaching chemistry for almost four years. We had a new proper equipped laboratory built. As secondary pupils, we proudly wore pleated skirts instead of those boring pinafores. Felt hats imported from England were won on Sundays, otherwise, knitted caps were worn on week days, and ties with an emblem of some bird were worn daily.

How exciting it was wearing white home dresses on All Souls Day, a big Catholic day. On this day, we pray for the dead in Purgatory. That's where you spent time getting cleansed before going to heaven. Our prayers hasten the dead's stay in Purgatory. All Saints Day is for holy people in heaven. I cannot tell you how many acclaimed saints are up there. St Christopher protects travellers and St Jude helps the desperate. I would never have progressed had it not been for St. Jude. For his personal reasons, Daddy hated my new name Margaret even though I tried convincing him that a percentage of saints have that name and they are all my patron saints. The list went on and on. Daddy looked at me with piercing blue eyes and smiled, *"The nuns have really brain-washed you."*

One thing I was grateful for was that Daddy never criticized the Catholic Faith except the birth control business of which I had no idea what that was all about. Certain chapters in health Science were skipped. Daddy never used the words sex or pregnancy. Daddy warned us with; *never get yourself into a family way.* Mummy calmly cautioned us to, *"Keep your distance from men, otherwise, you will get pregnant."* We took it literally and stood at a distant as if men had the plague.

I remembered Daddy saying, *"Life is the process of what you learn from one person to the other-the good they do, how they cope with life's trials, and the daily trivial disappointments."* He talked a lot about the most difficult aspect of life about accepting people as they are and avoiding people who make life hell for others. I never thanked him for that. *I wish I had.*

Bjordal Mines Limited,
Kabale,
19th March 1964

My dearest daughter,

I received your letter of which I thank you very much. Due to pressing work, I did not go to Kabale until now and have sent a belated card to Berit, hope she gets it. I do not hear much from the other girls. I am sure they are busy with school work. Looks like everything is fine with you. Helene writes when she can. She loves it in England. As you know she too will complete her nursing training end of this year.

So, you have a male teacher? This is the first time to hear of that. Even I had lady teachers to begin with. Pity your American teacher has left. You had mentioned you enjoyed her lessons, except once when she hit a skunk when driving to Mangu, picked it and brought it to class for you girls to dissect and many of you threw up because of the smell. That was funny. Hope you enjoyed the dance at Mangu High School. You did mention you dance a lot every Sunday. It is good your modern Nairobi friends bring records. As I say Sister Anastasia is quite modern minded.

I am glad you have a new secondary section and a proper laboratory. Looks like Sister Anastasia is making some good changes.

Lots of love,
Dad

Holidays are more fun now. We spend two weeks with Mummy and two weeks with Daddy. It's now two years that I truly have a Daddy, catching up for lost time. Late but it was worthwhile. I had to bring friends over to meet Daddy and enjoy *heaven* as I did. Together we watched the clear crystal night skies amplified by the star lights bathing in the sky or sunsets painting the blue sky all shades of red, orange, yellow, purple trimming dark clouds with sharp bright outline. Friends now truly believe me.

Next day, when the sky is painted an incandescent white, we hiked up steep rocks swooping down dangerously. I took them into narrow caverns with shafts covered with damp mosses and ferns growing in the crevices. We listened to our voice resonating in the valley. My experiences taught me many things and I hoped others could have the opportunities to enjoy life as I did with my father in Africa .

In our rooms, we listened to rain rapping lightly at our windows. With heads out the window, we enjoyed sharp drops needling our face until it tingled.

Every morning, we inhaled pure air expanding our chest to the fullest. No more asthma for me. Most friends I brought to my *heaven* made no fuss about a few animal smells or wood smoke. I wanted this life to last forever. You honestly felt the closeness of God above and in the surroundings. His breathe is in the wind. For most of us, we believed God was enclosed and limited inside churches. It angered me when religious people used kneeling or praying the rosary as a form of punishment instead of a reverence to God.

The *heaven,* I was born in did not discriminate me from mingling with mountain people or patting smelly goats or sheep or chasing chickens; bare footed. I did not understand why the whites in Kenya marginalize Africans. My mind seemed like a cluttered closet that needed sorting out. Only Daddy could have done that for me but he was not always in my life. I felt like an intermediary between two separate parents.

The first term we had a handsome English student from the Royal University (Nairobi University) teaching us science. Every girl smartened up for this gorgeous man. After Mr. Reed left, another handsome blue-eyed dark Goan man with a thin moustache and a goatee looking like a teacher from David Copperfield's *Oliver Twist* came to teach. We overlooked his meanness only because of his eyes. I wondered how he'd look had he shaved. Our grades surprisingly shot up. Next term, *the* final term, was like doing the French roulette sitting for only six subjects. God help you if you failed in just one of them. Over the years, Daddy said, *"Learn to make precise decisions on your own; I will not always be there to help you."* So I made Novenas to Padre Pio for seven days to intercede to God for me to pass. *Padre Pio was not yet canonized a saint.*

By this time, my friend *brain* was thinking in English completely. I, no longer needed to translate from Kiswahili or Luganda into English.

> *Bjordal Mines limited,*
> *Kabale,*
> *10th June 1964*

My dear daughter,
Thank you for your wishes for my forty-ninth birthday. I understand you are miles from civilization just as I am. What is going to happen to you girls with so many changes of science teachers? I am surprised as

84

well as disappointed, you want to give up French. A pity your French nun left. It's an important international language in Europe. I learnt French in the Congo and spoke Afrikaans a little. You and Sylvia were doing pretty well. What happened? I hope Sylvia will continue with it since she wants to become an air hostess. I will send her to France when I make enough money.

Well, my dear, do the subjects you are comfortable with. As always, I sincerely wish you the best. So you have a little genius in your class? I believe you girls too, are gifted in so many ways. Not many people are that lucky. I am so sorry there were so much misunderstandings and obstacles in your young life. If you had started at an early age at Maryhill, you would have been way ahead as that little girl. I am not saying you have not done your level best; you have done amazingly well considering the setback you have had. I have great hopes in you Mandy. You should tell me more about this Holy priest, Padre Pio. My younger sister, Birgit is quite ill. Perhaps you can ask your holy priest to pray for the both of us.

Lots of love and good luck.

Daddy

I did intercede with lots of saints to help my supportive Daddy and his forty three year old ill sister.

Daddy was a young father yet he took his responsibilities diligently with three sets of children, ex-wives and three hundred workers. Daddy was truly my rock as I wrote in my first book. Although he had plenty of problems, he never imposed them upon us. He made me very comfortable, always encouraging me to speak up and open my heart.

As stated earlier, Daddy hated makeup. *"Don't look like painted dolls,"* he'd say. Anyway, I let him know the nuns invited beauticians to the school. What an excitement that was. I wanted to volunteer to have my freckled face made up but shied away. Sylvia, had such a beautiful clear skin, but had no patience to sit still and have someone meddle with her face, even now at sixteen. One of her best friend, a mixture of Kikuyu-English from a lower form, was picked.

When I first came to the White Sister's School I was sadden to learn that darker skin siblings were sent to an African school next door. My Daddy who believed in education rather than skin colour would have gone berserk if we were separated. Dark complexion Goans or Seychellois were kept at the school, mainly because they were Catholics. I learnt as well this convent school was opened for orphans and coloureds.

Bjordal Mine Limited,
25ʰ July 1964

My dear Mandy,

Many thanks for your letter of 15th July. I am sorry I did not tell you my sister Birgit died a month ago on 25th of June.

I see that your school is becoming up to date with modernization. Well, quite honestly, I think my girls are beautiful. You definitely do not need to paint your faces as I have told you over the years. Some women over do it and yes, look like painted dolls. Do not mess your faces with these products for as long as you can help it. You will land up blocking your pores and getting acne and pimples.

I would never agree to separate you just because of shades of skin. I am surprised to see Catholics do that

86

and in Africa, mind you. I cannot believe the ignorance some white people have. Do they expect only light brown babies to be born of white fathers and African mothers? I noticed this behaviour in South Africa. Even a white child born in white family would be mistreated if they found out she/he had a drop of African blood four generations ago. Yet these new Dutch tribe called themselves Afrikaans.

Mandy, I have told you once and am telling you again there is nothing wrong with having freckles. Your Daddy is full them. When I make extra money, I will perhaps send you to America and have them removed. Look at beautiful actress Shirley McClain. She was once full of freckles. You are beautiful just as you are.

Lots of love to Sylvia and Berit,

Your loving,

Daddy

Daddy wrote back, pointing out indirectly, his experiences in South Africa. If a white child was born with slightly thicker lips, or had no moon at the bottom of their nails, or had dark curly hair, the government was stirred to study four generation of that family's genealogy. If found with even one percent African blood, the white family was humiliated and forced to live in African locations.

The nun called me to the office and asked me what my father was talking about. Stuttering, I explained that Daddy did not approve of the discrimination in Kenya. *It was the naked truth.*

Daddy gave us a surprise visit that year, 1964. The first visit since joining the secondary school; my *king* drove a white American Chevrolet.

87

Panicky sister Alfred gathered us shouting, *"Your father is here, your father is here."* I believe this nun was always nervous.

We were smartly attired in well pressed uniforms and polished shoes as trained by the nuns. Memories flooded my mind when Daddy visited us at Kisubi. Sister Felix's hands shook when she saw us disarrayed after being tortured in the forest with our hair dishevelled, faces red and smeared with mud and tears, and our hands blistered. The girls were ordered to scrub us clean, comb our hair and dress us in polka-dotted dresses with long forgotten shoes put on our feet.

Just like at Kisubi, we found Daddy seated in the parlour dressed in a black suit and tie, well-polished black shoes and he smelt of Old Spice. He stood up as we walked in. *What a gentleman he was.* We hugged and kissed. At Maryhill, we were left to our privacy and we talked without fear. First thing Daddy asked us about was our diet. We gave him a week's menu and he smiled. Talkative me mentioned we missed Marmite and Bovril. My Daddy jotted that down. I told him I was nervous about the coming exam next term. Daddy assured me that Sanatogen in hot milk would help calm us during our finals.

After almost an hour, Sister Anastasia came and had a private talk with Daddy. She said the school couldn't provide Marmite or Bovril but she would rather give the whole school permission to bring one bottle if we wanted. The fourth formers were privileged to drink hot Sanatogen before going to bed during Cambridge examination.

Having heard wonderful stories about my handsome, adventurer, musician, pilot, and writer

88

Daddy, my friends excitedly surrounded him wanting to hear the deep voice I talked about.

"Doesn't he look like Pat Boone?" whispered a friend behind a cupped hand. A few friends questioned Daddy about his African travels and that sparked him to talk about his adventures. Not wanting to be the centre of attention, he in turn asked them about their fathers. Many said they were farmers in Nakuru, Naivasha, Meru or Athi Rivers.

Come August, we were in evergreen mountainous Uganda. Daddy took us out to dinner and introduced us to many business friends. The conversation dwelled on how well Sylvia was doing and I was a little behind. I wished the-earth-would-open-up-and-swallow me. *How could you do this to me Daddy?* I was thankful Mr. Wilkinson, Daddy's lawyer, diplomatically overlooked the comment. I was already an introvert; very conscious about being two years older than my classmates. Sylvia, an extrovert, participated in conversations of law and business giving her opinion. I could never do that. I had learnt a thing or two about modesty from nuns unlike my opinionated sister. There and then, I decided to prove Daddy wrong as I had done with teachers. I believed Daddy had forgotten I went to school late. Despite that I still loved my Daddy.

I wrote back 5th October 1964, indirectly inviting Daddy to our big Parents Day. Daddy must see me give a yearly school report. I will not die on the stage. Over a month I had thoroughly rehearsed and memorized the speech under Mrs. Parson's encouragement and supervision. Her husband, the school manager, reminded me so much of Daddy. He once shot the biggest python we ever saw; much larger than those horrible snakes at the Nairobi Museum.

There was pin drop silence when I began my speech; pausing and looking at the audience after every end of a long sentence as I was instructed to. That made me stutter a little but I stilled myself and continued. I bowed and was applauded.

Backstage I changed into a long-trailed dress over a can-can. I was the main character in the play. Without my glasses, I saw nobody. I unbelievably transformed into a sophisticated aristocrat lady shocking Mrs. Parson, the nuns and my classmates. That was the first and last play I ever participated in, vowing never to act. Sylvia said I had a standing ovation. It was hard to believe her sometimes.

Determined to earn a few distinctions, I memorized St. Marks Gospel, Church history and Shakespeare's Macbeth by heart; something I believed was an impossibility. At least, I was confident with Art. The rest of my subjects were on the border-line of passing.

After the nuns did their last round, many girls crammed under their blankets using flashlights to revise. I needed my sleep. I once tried doing that trick, next day I was so exhausted I messed up in the test. Although I was anxious about finishing school I was terrified to face this vast world. *The outer world was full of every kind of wickedness* was all we heard from the nuns. How I wished there was a world, like our *heaven* where I felt protected and at peace. Perhaps the nuns meant colonial Kenya was like that; perhaps the nuns experienced terror during the World Wars. I should ask my open-minded Daddy. He knew the world history to the minutest detail.

Bjordal Mines Limited,
Kabale,
15th October 1964.

90

My dear Mandy,

Thanks for your letter of 5th October. Do you see what determination can do for one? With no one to trust at the mine, I am sorry I could not attend your end of the year concert. I would have been the proudest father there; applauding and letting everyone know that you were my daughter. Helene should be back from England next month. I am sure you girls are just as anxious as me. I hope she gets a job at Mulago hospital. I am proud of you, as well, for bravely giving a speech to parents. Do not worry about your hands shaking. That is quite normal. It happens with adults even. You say your English manager looks like me? Oh well he might be a far cousin. I have told you the Vikings ruled England at one time. Royalties came to Europe to find wives for their kings as well. We have British soldiers buried in Norway as well as many Norwegians who died when Norway had great famine. People died by the thousands.

I am sure Sylvia was right about the standing ovation. Parents of other children must have heard how shy you were and wanted to encourage you.

I am coping pretty well on my own, always wishing you girls were here with me. The good thing is I will be seeing you in December all done with schooling, at least for the time being. Time has gone so fast. Just a couple of years back, you could not write in English. Now you are better than I am and your spoken English is excellent as far as I am concerned.

Love to Sylvia and Berit,

Daddy

I truly understood how lonely Daddy was living like a hermit up that beautiful mountain. I bet even the wonderful surrounding waterfalls, rivers, a sky full

91

birds, and the sounds of night creatures could not lull him to sleep. Even monks have people around the monastery. Daddy worked late into the night. *Sometimes he read himself to sleep.* During the day, he never took an hour's break. He could have gone home, had lunch, taken a short nap and gone back to work. I believe Daddy had a little stubborn streak and certain things triggered his temper.

At this time, I did pretty well health-wise but weird, painful lumps appeared on my back and neck. I went to the infirmary for treatment but the nun in charge wasn't there. Unfortunately Sister Anastasia offered her assistance.

"Let me have a look at them," she said confirming that at least they weren't *mango worms.* Every day of the week she changed the bandages. It took almost a month before the lumps subsided.

> *Bjordal Mines Limited*
> *Uganda,*
> *27th October 1964*

My dear Mandy,

I have just received a letter from Sister Anastasia that you are ever falling ill and has come to a conclusion that you are near nervous breakdown due to the coming examinations. She asked me if I minded you do not sit your examination papers.

It's alright dear. You do not have to strain yourself. You have worked so hard. You do not have to kill yourself. I understand. Most importantly I want you to be healthy. You had done remarkably well all these years. I am a little confused. I do hope you feel better.

> *Lots of love and kind wishes,*
> *Daddy*

I posted a letter through the day students explaining everything. Sister Anastasia heard a group of girls, including my little friend, Sylvia C, giggling in the locker room. I ignored them and rushed back to class after excusing myself at the new flush toilets. There below the stairs stood Sister Anastasia and my heart skipped a beat.

"Margaret what is all that noise I hear in the locker room?"

"I don't know," I said.

"Well. You should. You are Head Girl!" She commended. She asked me what test I was doing. I said Geography.

"In that case you shall lose half the marks on the paper." She said pouting off. Daddy questioned me why I was almost third last in class. I dare not tell Daddy the truth: he would have blown his head off.

What on earth have I done to Sister Anastasia to deserve this? She had been after my blood for quite some time. I had even avoided communicating with her as Head-girls are supposed to do. By golly, I will not give up just a couple of weeks before the exams.

Maryhill School,
Thika, Kenya,
4th November 1964

My dear Daddy,

How could Sister Anastasia write to you about such an important issue without consulting me? I knew this would happen after the daring letter you wrote to her. She has not forgiven you. Its years since I've been to the infirmary for medical help I am so much stronger now than I've ever been. She insisted on treating the boils even though that was not her duty.

93

Can I not sit for the exam because of three little boils? You have already paid for my papers from Cambridge and Oxford University. I bet they have already arrived. Supervisors from England are already in Nairobi to invigilate us. Daddy I am sitting for the examination even if it kills me. Last year, Shirley had mumps and her papers were taken to her at the infirmary. Lorna C got measles her papers were taken to her.

Daddy, I am going to get this letter posted to you by a day pupil Indian friend of mine and will send you another through the school, just as a precaution.

> *With lots of love,*
> *Your loving daughter,*
> *Margaret*

I wrote another letter and confidently handed it to Sister Anastasia. She never mentioned writing to Daddy nor asked me if I were sick. She probably thought I had agreed not to sit for my examination. What was she to do with my papers from England? I was curious to know. It's November, for crying out loud. I had spent nine years of my life at this school only to drop out a month before the final stage. I may be timid but not crazy. I still had that simplicity mind of a child, easy to forgive and forget. Sylvia would have fought tooth and nail and caused drama with the nun. Even at seven years old, when Sylvia was once slapped across the face and her nose bled; she smeared it all over her face and shouted, " *I shall tell my Daddy you slapped me and made my nose bleed*". Daddy had taught me *never to argue with a fool. Let them believe in their foolishness.* We lost our young school manager to cancer. What a blow that was.

Bjordal Mines Limited,
Kabale, Uganda,
14th November 1964

My dearest daughter,

I am glad Sister Anastasia is taking good care of you and has taken time to press out whatever was in your body. Yes, I too suspect it must be these mango worms. They are quite a pest and painful. It is nothing to worry about really. If you happen to sit outside somewhere, a fly can just lay its eggs on you for nourishment. Crafty wicked pests, I tell you. Remember the science book I showed you when you visited in 1963? Flies carry all sorts of ailments. The thing that needs to be done is to let the boil take its course then press out the dreaded worms. Something so minor like this might have made you miss a vital examination. Say thank you to Sister Anastasia for me.

I am sorry to hear the loss of your manager at such a young age.

It's amazing that all of my dear girls are doing serious examinations this year at different levels. I am the proudest father in the world. Best of luck.

My love to Sylvia and Berit,
Daddy

I stubbornly continued the overall duties expected of a Head Girl: distributing letters to the school, taking the girls in for supper, checking assigned chores, ringing the bell when I was supposed to and giving instructions without really using my voice. I was grateful Daddy taught me to be polite to the authority, no matter the circumstances

95

I told Daddy about my Novenas to Padre Pio in Italy. This priest had the five wounds of Jesus Christ and every Friday they bled and he had to wear bandages. I asked him to pray for me to get second grade. I know Daddy did not believe in such things.

Had I a first grade I would honestly have forfeited my life and become a Carmelite nun, like St. Teresa. Then I thought about my Daddy's reaction, " *You are throwing your precious youth to be locked up in a convent?* " What about my Muslim family? I should have seen a priest for advice but I did not. But, there was still plenty of time ahead of me.

Bjordal Mines Limited,
Kabale, Uganda,
24th November 1964

My dearest Mandy,

Your letter of 1st November really cheered me up. I cannot, for the life of me imagine Sylvia sitting still and knitting. But I suppose with practice and determination she will get there. But please advise her, for me, to study and do revision instead. You will soon be sitting for a vital examination.

You spend a whole week plucking flowers and decorating paths? Isn't that a waste of time and flowers? Oh well, I suppose the nuns know what they are doing. Moreover, they do have plenty of flowers.

You are wise to sleep when it's time to sleep. That is very important. Study as much as possible when its daylight. The brain tends to get exhausted when over worked. Unfortunately for me, I cannot sleep some evenings. I read until I finally manage a few hours of sleep. I suppose that's because I'm now forty nine years old. Age does that to some individuals.

You must tell me more about this Padre Pio. Even if I do not believe in miracles, scientific things do happen. Let's see if you get a second grade. Why did you not ask for a first grade? I am so happy you are well and looking forward to sitting for your examination. You have made me a very proud father. I hope the nuns have given your class Sanatogen as I had suggested before going to bed. You do not have to be nervous. Tell Sylvia and Berit the same.

Best of Luck and prayers,
Daddy

With my Daddy finally praying, I should get by.

Daddy's letter arrived after the Cambridge and Oxford examinations had started two weeks now. I attacked the papers with vengeance to prove to the headmistress how wrong she was, scaring me to death and getting Daddy on her side.

Prince Henry, who was educated in England twenty years earlier helped me with literature. I got the highest merits, *Distinction.* Doing the English grammar paper was like doing the Russian roulette. You either pass or you fail the entire year's work. Failing meant no university or getting a job. If you are lucky the school may allow you to sit the whole exam again another year, *that is if you were younger: 17 years or so.* Sylvia had never been this serious before.

Bjordal Mines Limited,
Kabale,
Uganda,
25th November 1964.

My dear girls,

By the time my letter reaches you will probably be through your examinations. Helene is back from

England and I understand the family is coming over to see you. She looked very smart and has an English accent. I am glad the Sanatogen helped calm you down, hope it helped the rest of the class. I am glad Sylvia and Berit are serious. That is a good sign. You know it will soon be over. We shall have a good holiday thereafter, I promise.

I will not write much and you do not have to reply, I understand. We have plenty of time for a long chat later.

Best of luck,
Dad

What a time we had growing up. There were no BEST OF LUCK cards, let alone Daddy's encouraging letters arriving on time. But we coped with reality pretty well.

Quite aware of school payments, children worked hard to show gratitude to our slogging fathers. Daddy shopped our essentials for three months: tubes of Maclean toothpaste, Lux bath soaps, bars of washing soap, Brylcreem, three pairs of socks, more knickers, vests, petticoats and a pair of white sheets and pillow cases which we washed weekly. No one ever forgot to mark or sew our names on our comb, hairbrush, tooth brush, towels, facecloth, and socks. Extra items were kept under lock and key at the linen room. Some of us sneaked in a forbidden mirror, vanity was a sin needed to be confessed. The text books and school stationary was provided by the school; paid for by parents. Later on, we had what was called a 'tuck- shop' with sweets and biscuits which we moderately bought on Sundays.

Daddy's letter of 25th November arrived sooner than expected; the last letter to me as a pupil. We were doing our last art paper, 'Still Life,' when Helene and the family arrived. The school was as quiet as expected; you could have heard a pin fall. Suddenly the girls downstairs shouted, "Sylvia, Margaret; Helene is here," and all sorts of comments and giggles. My concentration was gone. I rushed through the painting and left before anyone. Sylvia seriously continued. You know, she loved art. Helene wore a red blouse with a black, tight skirt and looked absolutely stunning. I was so proud of her. She had an English accent, too. I believed I was finally free. Time to work and support myself.

Daddy was home the first week of our arrival. I waited with anticipation as Daddy joyously read out our results. I had gained a second grade. *Thank you Padre Pio.*

Off we went to the mine and had so much fun: dancing, picnicking in the wilds, riding on lakes flooded with hippopotami and sleeping in tents right in the depths of the Impenetrable Forest of Uganda. The rain poured like a waterfalls and thunder shook the earth beneath us. Angry gods sent threatening lightening across the blackened sky, the zigzag flashes keeping us tightly cuddled together.

How I silently wished Daddy's sons were here to enjoy this. They have been away in Norway, I believe since beginning of 1963, with probably three short visits. Like us, they had been to an English school in Eldoret or Nakuru, Kenya when very young. Daddy said the English did not treat them fairly, therefore, Ulfhild took them to Norway. I wanted to ask Daddy more questions about my brothers but he hardly brought up the subject. So I left it at that.

My first Communion 1957

CHAPTER SIX
OFF TO COLLEGE

How gratifying it was being treated like a responsible mature individual in college. I had my own very clean room with a writing desk and roomy closet. Directly opposite me was a communal bathroom with showers shared by all first floors. The tutors were mainly English and Scottish besides Africans, a Khoja, a Hindu and a Goan. Almost all lived in the complex, each responsible for one floor. We had a lovely American tutor, wife of a minister, Akumu, whom I thought was a Somali. They had the cutest little two year old daughter.

After a couple of months, a tutor asked me if I go to hairdressers regularly; as I had a new hair style every day. Some even asked if I used wigs. They are yet to see Sylvia's or Helene's amount of hair! Daddy joked that he was balding because we took all his hair. I overlooked the annoying questions from tutors. They jolly well knew we aren't allowed out of college premises during the week. In any case, I had no money to throw away at hairdressers or the patience to have someone figuring out what to do with my long hair. What with ten shillings pocket money every Friday, enough for bus fare to church, or to go for a movie. End of the month, we got forty shillings. Sylvia and I were grateful the Kenya Government paid for the nursing and teacher training. A great help that was to my sick Daddy.

I made new friends quickly; otherwise, coming from a convent school, I'd be stuck in college for good. My three best friends were a Sikh, a Bohora and a Hindu. I learnt everything about them as Daddy wanted

101

me to including their religions and culture. I had so much fun dressing like them, attending Indian weddings, religious feasts, and enjoying their tantalizing foods! They were fun whilst Maryhill girls were my family. I couldn't wait for Sylvia to join me in September.

Bjordal Mines Limited,
Kabale,
19th January 1965

Dear Mandy,

You tell the tutors you got your hair from your Daddy. There is nothing wrong with what they say. It shows they are admiring you and wish they had some of it. Generally speaking, many English and Europeans have scanty hair. By golly, you girls do have an enormous amount of hair; I must admit that myself. I too, had plenty of hair.

I am glad you are settled at college interacting with every tribe from India besides the different tribes in Kenya. I am sure you will learn a lot about their countries and cultures and even try their tantalizing foods. I'm glad you find college a whole exciting world. I'm sorry you miss your old school friends. Remember you had a strong bond almost like one big family; practically a tribe of your own, with white fathers and African mothers. You are a new creation. Be proud of that. I believe one day people in the world will interact more and accept each other. I am sure the bond you had will last forever. At least you have met Vera and she takes you out on Saturdays. Don't tell me these English and Scottish tutors are narrow-minded worse than the nuns? I thought you would be freer in college, not isolated as in the convent schools. I hope you will start dating soon.

I wish you a lot of luck and happiness.

Love Daddy

Sylvia specifically came to college for me to untangle her shrunken hair. As I gently brushed it, she complained about her nose even though Daddy said his family had big noses. We could never put ourselves down when Daddy lifted us up. If any daughter out there in the world does not believe in a father's love; it does exist. I thanked Daddy for his letter of 19th January. He was very particular about me dating. So I made sure to let him know I dated my college mate's brothers. When noticing how miserable girls in love were I was on guard. I did not want to go down misery lane. Daddy had said *earn your certificate, get a job, have a saving then marry at twenty-five at the earliest.* My Daddy knew what he was talking about. I believe he regretted rushing into marriages.

I told him that now the tutors have become friendly. Having instilled confidence in me, I opposed some of the lectures. We had a debate on the importance of education and civilization. If we thought it contrary, we were to give our views. I was the only one who opposed civilization; pointing out that the Maasai in Kenya and the Hima at Kabale lived in perfect harmony with nature. They knew the goodness of herbal medication and ate healthy diets. Many educated people changed their culture and no longer spoke their mother tongue. Some Africans laughed at me when I spoke to them in Kiswahili. They kept answering me in English. My Daddy brought us up speaking in Kiswahili; he learnt it from Mummy. Anyway, I got an A despite verbal arguments and oppositions from peers. Our literature tutor, Mrs. Dudgeon, asked us to write a thesis on Egypt. As luck would have it, magazines in a huge city council bin caught my eyes. There I was rummaging inside for discarded magazines and to my joy I found the story of Cleopatra.

Having read an article Daddy wrote in some magazine about his journey from Haugesund, Norway down the Mediterranean across the River Nile through Egypt and the Sahara stimulated me. Practically every scene of the movie with Elizabeth Taylor and Richard Burton was there. I cut pictures out, pasted them and varnished them with clear nail polish. I probably wrote a whole black cover book.

Daddy looked forward to hearing from me. We both worried if our letters were late. Our Australian half-brother often wrote to his father. Daddy had tons of his letters filed. He wished the other girls would write once in a while. Politics in Uganda were taking a serious turn of events, otherwise, everything seemed fine. Although I had lived in the convent schools nine years; I could not imagine myself standing in Daddy's shoes, totally alone. At least, I had over two hundred girls going through the same life as me. In college, I was again surrounded by plenty of people.

Bjordal Mines Limited,
Kabale,
29/3/65

Dear Mandy,

How are you, my dear? We are all up here at the mine now and miss you terribly. The girls did not seem to like it in Kampala so they turned up one night with George when he came back.

It's a real problem as I do not know what to do with them being busy at the mine. You know what it is

104

like. They have not planned what to do with themselves and that cannot work in this cruel world. Although the nuns have done a good job with your morals but telling you that 'money is the root of all evil,' and 'cursed be the rich for they will not enter the kingdom of God and blessed are the poor they will inherit... They misinterpret the Bible, I am sorry to say. If you work hard and rightfully earn your dues, take care of yourself and family I do not see what is wrong with earning money. God helps those who help themselves.

Half a ton of Tantalite-Columbite ore disappeared from the mine. You know my place, you have to cross a dangerous dam on a floating bridge, no one has a car here but the manager and me. How did a whole ton disappear leaves one to wonder. I have lost a lot of money, Mandy. But what to do?

As you know, George is still working for me. I wish that Helene had worked at Mulago for some time. She had worked at Nsambya Hospital before I sent her to England.

Helene, the poor girl is so much in love with George I hate to part them. She could still work in Kampala and come visit him when she gets time off.

I am struggling worse than ever at the mine because Wolfram price has dropped. Congratulations on your work and you are right about everything you said, I am very proud of you.

You have a lot of sense and initiative; I hope life will treat you fairly.

May the Good Lord bless you my dear,

Daddy

Again, Daddy sent me God's blessing! I could not believe that. I often wished to hide in a shell like a tortoise but Daddy's constant encouragement helped me interact with people of all races and culture.

I was so puzzled about the mysterious theft that took place at the mine. Probably James Bond would have found the culprits. How could anyone do that to my Daddy when he worked so hard?

I wrote back how sorry I was to hear what was done at the mine. It had to be planned by someone who worked there. Daddy had the key to the store. You needed plenty men to load the heavy Wolfram onto a lorry and to cross that unsteady bridge. The lorry had to be pushed silently across the floating bridge so no echoes went up the mountain to alert Daddy.

To cheer Daddy up I told him I was in the tennis and gymnastics clubs even though I was uncoordinated and clumsy; only because he said it would improve my health. I envied the Goan students taking all the Golden Awards. Daddy would have proudly hung mine in the lounge up in *heaven; had I achieved any.*

As Daddy was opened minded, I mentioned a girl had an abortion at the college and I nervously visited her. After recovery, she was thrown out of college. Many African girls had babies taken care of by their mothers. That was scandalous and shocking at this time.

Daddy once told me, "*Once you hold that paper in your hand nothing in the world matters.*" There was no shortage of teachers in any part of the world. I resolutely decided to persevere many trials and emotional pain that one often gets. Dealing with unstable politics was frightening. Daddy stayed calm though he knew what I was going through. He diverted my mind about how dressing professionally was important and having a good aptitude helped one in the world. He never talked much about being overly

106

wealthy but more about *wasting and over spending.* The church called those deadly sins.

Bjordal Mines Limited,
Kabale, Uganda
2nd *April 1965*

My dear Daughter,

Many thanks for your letter of 26/3/65 of which I was very pleased to receive. Do not ever say you are parentless. You are lucky to have both parents who love you. This is why Mandy I keep drumming into you girls to be careful when going out with boys. Your church forbids birth control. It's very sad to say this girl committed murder as far as I am concerned. Be careful Mandy.

I note that you like college and that you are healthier with the physical exercises and games that you do. Of that, you can best rest assure will help you with decisions you make in life. I am glad you are learning new subjects. Psychology is vital when dealing with children.

You do not say when you are coming to Kampala. Your sisters seem to know but me. Helene and George are together at the mine. Sylvia and Berit as well adore George. I must admit he is quite charming and good looking and seems reasonable. I only see Sylvia and Berit in the mornings before I leave for work. In the evening, up to seven at night, they are still at Helene and George's house. Poor Helene seems to be working hard as a housewife. Sylvia and Berit read, eat, wash their clothes and sleep. I wish I had such a life.

I have no idea what to do with your sisters as I go to work early and am out the whole day. I want them to practice typing and painting. I have to take them to Kampala and see what they can do. It is a great

107

disappointment as Sylvia in particular is very talented and intelligent.

I took Berit to the Entebbe Aerodrome without success. To my great disappointment just as I was going to sell my stock of Wolfram and had already shipped out five tons; the price dropped to nothing. What is going to happen now I really do not know? I supposed the Bank will not give me any more credit, and then everything will have to stop. I have workers to pay, bills for all my boys still in school, money to send to Australia, money to send to Ulfhild in Norway. I still feel obligated to even your mother.

To cheer you up my dear; Sylvia turned eighteen on thirty first of March and we had a party at George's house. What I noticed about Sylvia is that she is a wonderful dancer and is very charming. Berit is still a big baby at times. Mandy, do not ever say you are parentless. Both your Mother and I are here for you, remember that. Well this is for now, Meg. Hope to see you soon.

Lots of love

Daddy

I was hurt when Daddy said my sisters knew of my arrival but not him. Daddy confided in me that he did not know what to do with my sisters. As far I was concerned, we needed that break after years at convent schools. Daddy wanted Sylvia to do typing or paint instead of idling time away. Overall, he had fun with his daughters around. Eventually, we all streamed out to our own destination and he became a lonely man. Daddy had a soft spot for Helene. True to his words, Helene always honestly worked hard. On visiting friends' married sisters, I found being a housewife was hard work. Marriage was definitely out of the question for me, at least for now. The women in Daddy's life had it easy with plenty of domestic help. That was how life was for women when I was growing up. They did not work but run a home.

Daddy's letter arrived at college during the holidays. Believing I was adopted by the nuns; Miss Hall sent it to Maryhill. The nuns re-addressed it to Uganda, unopened!

I was sorry the bank refused to loan Daddy money. Once banks hear of business failing they avoid you like a plague. My Daddy was an honest man. He would definitely have paid them back once the business picked up. The Bjordal Mine had done exceptionally well over the years. Exportation of Wolfram and Tungsten reached its peak in the fifties and sixties due to Daddy's patience and credulity of training three hundred very simple workmen. Africans in Uganda underrated the Bachiga. *They were uneducated and uncivilized.*

The government looked up to him bringing them money in taxes. Daddy's mines were four hundred and thirty five miles southwest of Uganda and the Great lakes between Uganda, Rwanda and the Congo Democratic Republic.

His main concern was his Australian and Norwegians sons still in school. I wished once in a lifetime Raymond would meet his father. I really did. Raymond would have loved Daddy as I did. I was happy Daddy had fun on Sylvia's birthday. She definitely was a good dancer and an excellent ballerina. You would not get me to even try on a ballet costume even though dancing is my passion. All in all, Maryhill engraved the importance of morals; Kisubi taught me never to trust anyone; Highridge Teacher Training made me become bolder and esteemed. My destination

109

in life was to see that children are happy. At least the time they were with me. That's what God called me to do.

Bjordal Mines Limited,
Kabale, Uganda,
20th April 1965

My Dear Mandy,

Thanks a lot for your letter and Easter greetings. I was very disappointed you did not come here (Mine). Well, never mind. George, Helene and I are going down to Kampala before end of the month and we hope to see you before you leave for Nairobi.

My car mysteriously went down the hill. Someone must have got the wrong end of the stick and pushed it down. That is very difficult to understand. Evilness seems to creep on me on all sides.

I am hoping Sylvia and Berit will find jobs when I take them back to Mother in Mengo. With my problems at the moment, I can't send Sylvia to a school in France as I had hoped to. But alas! Fate is against me these days. I am afraid the bank will not loan me money anymore. I am, therefore, very depressed. I was hoping to go to England for a heart operation, now it's out of the question.

Anyway, we all have difficulties, but experiences that I have had, take the worse in my life.

I look forward to seeing you in the weeks of 29th April to 1st May.

Lots of love
Daddy

I could have kicked myself for not seeing Daddy that holiday. I wasn't brave enough to travel alone three hundred and fifty miles. Daddy rushed down to

110

Kampala just as I was about to leave for Kenya. Even though Daddy looked great, I was afraid my Tarzan, my Hercules' life, was in grave danger. Who heard of operating on the heart? I had seen and felt the chicken, goat and cow's heart; it's a very red and tender organ with weird tubes. His heart must be similar, I thought. I left Uganda with a heavy heart. Unfortunately, I carried the malaria bug in me to Nairobi and was sick as a dog, as Daddy might have said. The matron changed my soaking wet night dress, sheets and pillow cases when the fever sky racketed, then used extra blankets when the body temperature dropped. Our Principal, Miss Hall, often checked on me. Sick as I was I still prayed for him, " *Please God don't take my Daddy away.* " The news of his heart condition hit me like a thunder bolt. I went through the denial stage. It cannot be true. I then comforted myself with the knowledge that Helene and George were there some twenty minutes down the mountain. As I said before, Daddy lived in complete isolation and austerity.

I heard Daddy's bass voice through his precious letters talking about the wretched flu and bugs yet nothing about his heart. He once wrote, *"I hope George will cope with the mine when I am gone."* I broke this big boundary between adults and children and asked him, *"Gone where?"* He wrote back, *"Mandy, there is nothing that can be done with my heart"*

When I went home, I was relieved to find Daddy still looking healthy and energetic. We excitedly packed picnic food and accompanied him to Itama and Rubugure forests. Daddy saw the oncoming rain storm and asked us to squash up in the front seat. Down came torrents of rain. Angry gods shook the car. Lightning, my greatest fear, almost struck the car. Daddy looked

111

sideways, amused at our cowardice assuring us we were safe in the car. The rain cleared as quickly as it had started. The air felt cold and damp. Pulling our jumpers overhead, we slithered on treacherous, shifting surfaces beneath our shoes, laughing exultantly. How excited I was to actually see the hut that Helene and I lived at when we were only babies.

"Your mother was about your age then," Daddy smiled. *(I* could not imagine my proud Mummy, a royalty, living in the midst of the wild) Would any woman in their right sense have done that?

When Daddy married his next two wives, he was a successful, rich man. A millionaire I believe. They did not live in huts nor darn his socks. Daddy said the Bachiga (Bakiga); a sturdy agricultural tribe had their own Kingdom and a fairly well organized simple government. Kigezi was formerly called Mpororo.

Daddy introduced us to many of his workers prospecting for gold in a water stream. What fun my friends Mary Brown, Elvira and I had feeling like explorers. I watched Daddy's expectations amidst gathered group of employees giving an account of what went on during his absence. Tiny particles of gold in bottles were handed to Daddy. I wondered if they were worth hundreds of workers for so little gold. I found great patience and simplicity in other parts of Daddy's complicated life. Inside the hut, as we enjoyed packed sandwiches; Daddy said, *"Your mother saved me from a python right at this hut."* There was a small wooden cupboard with tea leaves, sugar and a tin of Milkmaid. One man started a fire and the smoke took a convoluted circular path from a three stone, triangularly arranged, rising with the current of air right up to the tall trees and mingled with the low clouds.

112

Bjordal Mines limited,
Kabale, Uganda
20th May 1965

My dear daughter,

    Many thanks for your letter of May 13th. Yes, everyone seems to have the flu and malaria these days. At the moment, Helene is bugged up with it that she can hardly speak. I, too, had twinges of it but so far nothing serious. We are finally producing wolfram here but we have a lot of problems with the old machinery which needs replacement.

    The lovers (Helene and George) are getting on well. Helene is doing well as a housewife. God only knows if George will cope with the mine when I'm gone. Anyway, he is doing well so far. Helene walks down the mine to see him and brings him lunch. If he is not satisfied with my daughter, there must be something wrong with him.

    I do not recall your mother or Ulfhild coming down to see if I was alright or needed lunch: working twenty-four hours a day at times.

    I see your college rules have changed. You can stay out only up to 6.30 p.m? Good God! That sounds like a prison. I suppose the principal has her reasons.

    Helene and I have been to Kabale several times. She seems happy to get away now and again. George doesn't seem to like that. These Mediterranean' are jealous and possessive of their wives. They think they may meet some other nice boy. I had a pep talk with Helene about marriage. Well, this is all for now, Mandy.

    Best wishes to you from me and all here.

113

Love you, Daddy.
PS I will get Helene to write to a few words tomorrow.

I was rather flattered and felt like an adult when Daddy confided in me about my older sister. Mummy never talked about such things to younger siblings; we need not know what goes on with a married woman, not even a sister. Daddy and me were open with each other. Getting an answer from anyone as expected was tough. So with every letter I wrote, I asked about Helene.

I witnessed the goodness of his heart: nursing the sick on Sundays with ungloved hands, cleansing smelly old wounds with Dettol and applying Gentian violet on them. He told me how often he came across a hit and run victim on the side road and took him to hospital paying for everything. I could never do that. Nursing was never on my agenda. Travellers were afraid of thugs faking to be dead by the wayside yet my Daddy felt obligated to help. He could easily been killed and everything stolen from the car. Mummy often warned us of mishaps on lone highways.

I thanked Daddy so much for his letter of 20th May; letting him know what wonders his endless verbal and written encouragement did for me.

I couldn't wait for Daddy's rare present. I still wear the brown leather watch he gave me when I was little.

As I observed Indian friends calculating their expenditure, I learnt about being thrifty. Daddy advised me to learn a thing or two from people of all races, so I did. He once joked about how Jews trusted nobody not even their own family. When a Jew counted his money he was always on the watch. Daddy was funny. Nairobi was so much fun. I made friends with shopkeepers, shoemakers, tailors, and drycleaners. I began designing

114

my shoes and even Indian outfits, *sarwas*. Kampala is either too hot or too wet, the very cause of malaria and flu-bugs, as Daddy called them. I boosted Daddy with my daily happenings never thinking I'd bore him. My college mates all heard about my wonderful father.

Bjordal Mines Limited
Kabale
Uganda,
5th June 1965

My dear Mandy,

Thanks a lot for your letter of 23rd May 1965 and the birthday card. I have been in Kampala for a week in order to repair the shaft on the lead mill, which broke. On the way, I collected letters at Kabale. I got yours, together with one letter from your mother and Sylvia. I had visited them mainly because I am fond of Sylvia as she is both intelligent and well behaved. My friends in Kabale said both of you resemble me. That made me proud.

When I was in Kampala, I managed to sell my Wolfram and got 600,000 shillings. So I could afford to be generous and took Sylvia and Berit out to dinner and bought them new clothes, shoes and lots of food stuff. You will have a nice present on your birthday. I won't say what it is.

On Sunday, we were supposed to go out swimming at Entebbe beach but Sylvia and Berit found an excuse not to come.

You say you have been chosen as a Social Secretary for the college. Congratulations. You should be proud. I remember when you were little you were chosen as a class prefect and you were afraid to do it and I told you it will improve your personality. Then you became the

115

school's Head girl, remember? Now the college wants to choose you as the Social Secretary. You should be proud. If there's anything I can help you with, do not hesitate to let me know. I like and love you Mandy. You are a fine girl with good characters. I could send you a cash check to National and Grindley's Bank Nairobi for your teeth and eyes. Just sign it on the back. If not, I am sure the nuns can help you with getting it cashed.

With lots of love,
Daddy

Daddy doubted that he could go to Norway or England for a heart check-up because he had lost so much money. Anyway, I was so excited when Sylvia brought me Daddy's present. A tight-fitting red woollen dress bought from the famous English shop the Drapers. Off we went to the studio dressed in our presents and sent Daddy photographs with a letter of thanks. Maybe inhaling iron-ore or Wolfram dust was taking a toll on him. He just turned fifty years old in June for crying out loud.

To cheer him up, I wrote a little about my adventure as a social secretary. Miss Hall handed me six tickets for an English play at the theatre one evening and I thought I had to choose six girls including myself. She didn't make it clear that it was a lower class going. So I selected six of my classmates and we joined the girls. I felt really bad when we were turned out so we went to a movie instead. So that's where we landed and arrived about half an hour late. The guilty girls quietly slipped into their rooms. I begged the non-guilty party not to say a word, I'd deal with it. One coastal Muslim girl shook with fear in case she was expelled. I promised not to mention her name. I think the theatre called Miss

116

Hall enquiring why so many girls were sent instead of the given tickets. Anyway all went well. All was settled at the office.

My optimistic Hercules was going downhill yet he was prepared for an operation. How do doctors operate on an enlarged heart and make it smaller? I thought the doctor was telling him a tall-tale. Heart operation were unheard of at this time. Doctor Bernard of South African was experimenting on fixing the human heart.

Bjordal Mines Limited,
Kabale, Uganda,
7th July 1965

My dear Mandy

Many thanks for your letter of 27th May 1965. Not to worry Mandy. That is small time. Everyone makes mistakes. Ulfhild, unfortunately, has some strange mental illness. That is quiet a toll on me. Well, I do not feel too bad myself as long as I take tranquilizing drugs but feel awful when I cannot get them. I as well have inadequate supply of oxygen that's why you noticed the oxygen tank by my bedside. I have not had news from the doctor who was to do the operation on the heart in Kampala. I hear that he has just returned from leave. No doubt I shall soon hear from him.

Everyone has the flue, tonsillitis, aches or bronchitis. This time I have escaped it. The doctor at Kisoro is critically ill with these ailments.

I only have a cough and am practically deaf.

I have sent Sylvia money to do a typing course at a college in Kampala.

I will send you some pocket money to help you out whilst in college.

Lots of love,

117

Daddy

When I asked Daddy about the oxygen tank beside his bed he said it was for emergency, *"The higher you are the thinner the air,"* he explained. *"It's not a necessity for all people but I have one as a precaution."* I sometime felt breathless up the mountain. I guess constant asthma weakened my lungs. It was no big deal really. Daddy said childhood illnesses help one acquired a strong immune system. I began to believe I was pretty strong as my siblings.

I thanked him for the money. Telling him how excited I was opening an account at Barclays Bank and saving for a rainy day, as he said I should. Although I was awfully terrified of his coming operation; I asked nothing about it instead I asked if Ulfhild was still ill. I believe Daddy said she spent a year in a mental hospital in Norway.

I remembered the doctor he referred to in Kisoro. Generally speaking, white people had weak immune system to fight tropical diseases. Flu almost killed Daddy. I do not take it lightly either. At the most, mine lasts one week. I was sorry to hear about the cough and ear infection he had. That is painful. I experienced that when I had the mumps. Daddy advised me to do typing but it's time consuming and boring. I hope Sylvia perseveres.

My strong Daddy began suffering from constant colds and coughs. Such stressful ailments weaken your immune system. How I wished I could help Daddy but I couldn't. When I didn't hear from him for more than two weeks my mind went haywire. I felt deserted. In addition to dormant aches and pains, I developed a toothache. Instead of writing to Daddy, as I should

118

have, I asked big sister for money to pay Doctor Saramjee, a completely European looking dentist. Apparently his mother was white. Unfortunately, Daddy got hold of the letter and he was angry.

Bjordal Mines Limited,
Kabale,
14th July 1965

My dear Mandy,

I saw the letter you wrote to Helene and George and I noted you asking them for money, saying no one bothers to write to you. Don't do this, Mandy. You know, Mandy, we all look up to you as a sensible girl and are watching your progress with great expectations and hope. I am hoping you will be able to cope with every situation in this world. Don't say you are happy one minute and miserable the next. I agree that it is a very difficult time you are going through. But think about poor Helene who was in England for two years by herself. You are not far away. Anyway, I'm glad you are working hard and learning so many more new subjects especially child psychology. Remember, knowledge is power.

Today I had a row with an Askari (majordomo) on the mine. He was needling me the whole day for an advance. Eventually, I let him have a hell of a racket. It was a Sunday and there I was working my guts out filling a submerged part of the road in the swamp. I wasn't in a good mood. You know, the echoes here in the mountains; they must have reached Helene and George. Later on, I was invited at their home for dinner.

I know you say you don't want money from me but here is two hundred shillings.

With best wishes and love,

119

Daddy

Daddy's letter hit me like a hammer on the head. I should have continued opening up to him no matter the circumstances instead of involving my sister. My intention was to avoid adding more stress on him. Daddy could not fathom how lonely I sometimes felt at college. That was the last time I ever asked for help from anyone but Daddy.

I thanked Daddy for the two hundred shillings giving him an account of how I spent it. Dr. Saramjee extracted my back tooth. I believe he used pliers!

I was turning twenty and yet he still worried about my health and safe arrival at college. I felt independent at that age except dealing with unpredictable issues. Are Norwegians different? Daddy was concerned about us even after we married. Daddy proved you do not necessarily need to be with a loved one to care about them.

Nyamolilo Mines,
Kabale, Uganda,
3rd September 1965

Dear Mandy,
Many thanks for your letter of 18th August 1965. Yes I got a letter from your college inquiring about why you had not returned to college. Anyway, I knew then that you are there now. So I did not answer them.

I am relieved to hear that you are well again. These wretched flues are a nasty piece of work. My shamba-boy, Masharubu, came staggering asking me for Dawa. He looked as sick as a dog. Do you know why he is

120

called Masharubu? It is because of his luxuriant moustache.

Don't worry about not writing to me often. I understand quite well how busy you are, and how much time you need to spend on your studies and your personal problems.

George had his car stolen in Kampala. Anyway, he brought a half-caste F. Wagg to work as a mechanic at the mine.

I am going to Kampala with F. Wagg, Helene and George. Mr. Wagg needs to attend a court case.

You need to fix that tooth, Mandy. Maybe remove the nerve. I had to do that with mine.

You must be excited your sister will be in Nairobi soon. You must take care of her and of each other. Do that for me, Mandy.

Bye, bye for now and lots of love from,
Daddy.

Daddy had never used the word bye before and that made me rather concerned. Was he sending me a hidden message without saying it directly? I prayed hard to stay sane. I forgot all about Padre Pio after doing the Cambridge School certificate. He would have interceded with Jesus to help my Daddy. We had no home telephones in those days otherwise I would have called Daddy at least once a month.

I discarded my friends now that Sylvia was in Nairobi. Nairobi Hospital treated nurse-students as adults unlike me at college. A good thing the college took a liking to Sylvia and I was able to go out alone with her. Once, I invited her to the tennis tournament. Faking I was ill, I asked the tutor if Sylvia could play in my place. Well, our team won. Again, I had no idea

121

what to do for the talent show so Sylvia performed ballet and the Tutors highly applauded her. As said earlier on, Sylvia was my hero and I was extremely proud of her rather than being envious or jealous. I thanked God for giving me such a gifted sister.

That November I had my practical finals at St. Peter Claver School, a city council school. Nearly sixty children between the ages of six to ten were crammed into one small classroom! I could hardly breathe nor teach unruly children. Many were quite dishevelled and spoke only Kikuyu, a language I hardly spoke-let alone understood. I almost gave up but dear old soul, Mrs. Dudgeon, sat at the back of the class, file in hand and a pen smiling and nodding her head in encouragement. If not of her, I would have failed. Mrs. Dudgeon heartedly congratulated me.

At recess time, a child's scream caught my attention. When I asked the staff what this was all about. They casually informed me this was the time the Headmaster disciplines naughty children. "Does anyone say anything?" I asked. They did not want to lose their job I was told. I walked up to the office and there lying across a table was a little boy being slashed with a soft thin green stick by the Headmaster.

"Why not a smack the child on the hand instead of whipping him?" I dare asked the dumb-founded man. Members of the school silently stared at me wondering who was I to oppose the head of the school. I cannot even bare a child crying. Will physical punishment in schools ever be abolished? I hope so.

Bjordal Mine limited,
Kabale, Uganda,
18th October 1965

Dear Mandy,

122

Many thanks for your letter of 10/10/65. You write of flu and tonsillitis. You are not the only one I can assure you. I have been in Kampala and everybody is suffering from the wretched flu one way or the other. I've picked it myself and was as sick as a dog. And it caught my tonsils as well. I am getting better but poor Festo!! He was so sick; he temporarily went mad running round the bus like a mad man. The miners tied him up with ropes. The virus had obviously attacked the nervous system.

I am glad you girls are keeping together. I am so pleased Berit is doing well. I always thought she'd be the problem child; I guess I was wrong. Parents want to trust their own children with the choices they make in life.

You say a thug snatched your bag going to church. You should have kicked him where it hurts most. You know what I mean. These goddamned thieves, they are all over the place.

I am glad you stood up for the poor child.

Kind regards to you and be more careful next time. If you see Sylvia and Berit give them my love.

> *Regards and love,*
> *Daddy*

My Indian friends dared me to dress in an exotic sari to church, the most uncomfortable thing I have ever done. I was nervous the outfit would slip off my hips. Luckily, there weren't many people around as it was a Sunday. I managed to elegantly get off the bus when a thief ran off with my handbag containing my return bus fair, a key to my room and a rosary in it. Anyway, I aroused looks at church, *an Indian in a Catholic church?* To make matters worse after mass, I had to walk about two miles in high-heels back to college!

123

Being Sunday, I held my tongue not to curse. I looked for matron Kairo for the extra key but she wasn't around. Mrs. Dudgeon kindly invited me to spend the day with her. We had a lovely lunch together, loving every bite of it.

That December, Daddy and I spent many evenings alone. He opened up my mind how Norway lived in terror during the Nazi's rule. People in Romania, Poland and even Germany went through hell.

"Sir Winston Churchill helped Norway, mainly due to the oil we had," he said. After moments of contemplation, he said, *"England lost ships faster than they built them."* Another moment of pause, he said, *"I'm not encouraging you to do this but, when Winston Churchill was bored with schooling or was often sent out of class he was inspired to draw exquisite arts and to write and is now known as a great writer and an artist."*

Being his cheerful self, Daddy played his accordion and we sang 'Oh Britannia,' an English patriotic song. My Grandma, who had studied at a British School, St Monica in Zanzibar, had taught me this very song when I was little.

> *Bjordal Mines Limited,*
> *Kabale, Uganda*
> *19th January 1966*

My dear Daughter,
Many thanks for your two letters. One from Mengo and one from Kenya. Sorry I have not been able to reply before due to pressing work. As you know, we are opening up the mine again and this calls for double work. We have to work day and night and Sundays, as well. I was terribly cheated by someone I trusted,

124

buying gold particles. The first time, they were genuine. Then this person conspired how to cheat me by coating stones with gold. So the second time, I did not bother to test them with acid as I normally do and handed the thief seven thousand shillings!

After being alone since 1963, Ulfhild is coming back in March to help me with the business. You know she is now the director.

I am sorry you experienced seeing a child hurt. Is there no place in Nairobi to report this? You look absolutely stunning and the dress fits you perfectly. I am glad you liked it.

I do hope you are well and in good spirits,

With lots of love,

Daddy

I was truly hurt to learn that Daddy lost plenty of money through fraud. Having lived in convent schools for eleven years, I believed in truthfulness. I held adult in high esteem yet I began to see deceitfulness. I, then, wrestled with myself not to be judgmental. That was a venial sin. Still, I disapproved anyone cheating my honest, hardworking Daddy. Imagine even my intelligent, Daddy was venerable to world's deceptions. I began to shun the world. I could have advised Daddy to do likewise but he would never have taken me seriously. I became more of an introvert. Always on the watch.

Daddy showed me a folder where he kept my letters pointing out how my sloppy handwriting had progressively improved over the years. I suspiciously asked Daddy if Ulfhild went through them, but he assured me she did not as he kept his secret files under lock and key on the right side drawer.

125

Daddy asked me why the English members of staff were picking on Sylvia. Actually the complaint was trivial. I doubted it was about being English or not but her hair. Regrettably, I laughed saying Sylvia was as white as any of them. Colonialism was slowly dying out after Independence in 1963. I, for one, did not care-two-hoots what anyone thought about me. Or hearing that blood mixture was abhorrent! Nobody knows me better than I know myself.

Daddy quickly wrote advising Sylvia, *"Tell the staff that you are half Norwegian, a quarter Arab and a quarter African of the royal family. That will make them think."* I loved my Daddy mostly for the simple ways he dealt with a situation. It was no big deal! We were fine just as we were. Other people were losers!

I remember one day, we watched him rubbing an African prickly plant, *kamwu,* on his bold patches. *"My workers told me these stimulate the cells and make the hair grow."* Sylvia exchanged a furtive glance and we smiled. Daddy never wore a hat although his crown barely had enough hair coverage.

Sylvia and I often exchanged Daddy's letters. He wrote more or less the same news really. At one time, I had asked Daddy not to type me letters like I am business personnel; so he wrote My Dear, Dearest and the like. Both Sylvia and I admired his handwriting so much we spent hours training ourselves to write like Daddy. Sylvia almost succeeded and I was close enough. I began noticing Ulfhild tiny messages at the bottom of his letters and wondered if she read our letters. I asked Daddy about that and he said only if she was at the office does he asked her to send a short message.

Bjordal Mine Limited,

Kabale, Uganda,
3rd April 1966

My Dear Mandy and Sylvia,

I was so glad to get your letter of 10th of April. I received it some time ago. I could not reply immediately as I was overworked and busy with so many problems. Good for you Mandy. Always stand for your rights for who you are.

I have been to Kampala in order to meet my wife who at long last has arrived and is at the mine. She asked me to send her kind regards to you.

The fact that Ulfhild has returned does not alter the matter of loving you and helping you, I assure you. You have never given me any trouble and I shall never forget that. You and Sylvia have worked hard and behaved yourselves with responsibility and wisdom. You sure must have got news for all that happened during Sylvia's stay here in Uganda. There are many things in the past that have disappointed me. I won't go through them again. Such is life. My wife is not a bad person and helps me with office work. I would like her to meet you.

Everything is going well at the mine now. I have a Seychellois fellow in charge of the mine, I must say he works ten times more than what I've been through with other managers just walking with their hands in their pockets, smoking cigars and complaining about almost everything.

I do hope you are well and doing fine dear.

With lots of love
Daddy
P.S. Kind regards from Ulfhild.

I remembered when I was only four years old going over to the car to say *Jambo* to Daddy's new mummy. I was completely ignored. Daddy later said Ulfhild was good doing our shopping in 1951. Daddy once brought us a perfumed liquid called *Light and Bright,* saying Ulfhild used that to keep her hair blonde. He said it would help retain my blonde hair too. The sun does that anyway. Can you imagine in all these years we have not met our half-brothers? My life would have been fulfilled if only I had spent one holiday with them when little. Daddy said he was sorry; Ulfhild would not permit that. I remembered so many puzzling things at age four and five. Oh well, I guess we shall finally meet her *without the boys around.*

> *Bjordal Mines Limited,*
> *Kabale, Uganda,*
> *3rd May 1966*

Dear Mandy and Sylvia,

Many thanks for your letters of 26th April which have just reached me. To start with your letter Mandy. I sent you some pocket money on 23rd April. Please let me know if you received it. You say I'm leaving Africa for good, don't worry. I will not leave you in the least. As I always told all of you, I shall have to go for a medical checkup sometime but I have no immediate plans. You also wrote about a parcel for Helene. As far as I remember, Helene received it. I think it had some clothes. About your photos, I would like to have them but if you want them back you could send me smaller ones please.

When looking at your letter Mandy, I see by the date you have already left for Kenya on 2nd of May. That is a pity; I wanted you to meet Ulfhild.

Now you Sylvia. It would have been better if you girls had let me know when you were coming to Uganda in good time. As it is with this wretched mail service I receive your letter ten days after you've written it. Would you like to come up to Kabale and stay with me? I shall be in Kampala sometime about the 14ᵗʰ-29ᵗʰ of May. When exactly are you leaving for Nairobi? Maybe you could get a lift to Kabale or come by the express bus. Then I could pick you. Ulfhild would be glad to meet you. What a pity Mandy had to go back to Nairobi. I would have loved to have seen you. Of course, I love you girls. I seem to get blamed for everything that goes wrong from the other girls. They have taken no notice of advices I give them of life in this wicked world. They don't take me seriously. I do not think the Convent School prepared you for facing the world. They probably did good religion wise but have made you totally naïve. I cannot realistically tell you what life is about and hope you take me seriously.

I don't know why you even think I want to leave you to fate. You have been very good girls.

As you know, I do nothing but work very hard and I have a lot of problems. Sylvia, if my letter for Mandy arrives in Mengo, please take it to her together with this letter. Let me know if you are coming.

Lots of love to you both,
Daddy

P.S. Please let me know Mandy if you want money or anything else. Ulfhild

That was a weird message from Ulfhild. No hello, nothing but money? Why would I ask someone who's never spoken to me my entire life for help? Sylvia and I never asked for money. Like any normal father, Daddy sent us pocket money at his own free will. The Kenya

Government provided us both with a bedroom, meals and pocket money every weekend and sixty shillings at the end of the month. That was quite sufficient. Daddy need not worry. Once I graduate, I will fully take care of myself.

Daddy should have been used to me coming home in April, August and December holidays. Sad to say, I did not see him that April 1966.

During some of those business trips with Daddy, I noticed his face turning red. Then he'd fall asleep at the wheels whilst driving and I'd gently tap him on the knee to awaken him. He would guiltily look at me with a smile and say; *"Mandy, do you think I was asleep?"* However, we took a break, had our picnic and continued our journey. I felt privileged sitting in the front with Daddy whilst Sylvia and my friends were in the back open van. When I went back to college, I forget how ill he was and wrote my inner feelings.

Bjordal Mines Limited,
Kabale,
24th May 1966.

My dear daughter,

I thank you for your letter of 14th May and note your comment that you are so unhappy. Now, my dear, let me tell you this. You should count your blessings and then you will find out that you should be happy and not otherwise. Quite so that your mother and I parted. But how many people in the world do you think have done the same under much worse conditions. Just think of those poor children who are brought into the world without even knowing who their parents are.

I have suffered as much as you children and perhaps even more missing you out here in the bush

130

when your mother took you away from me. It was only due to foolishness that we parted.

When I reflect upon my own childhood I could easily despair. My mother was very ill when I was very young. She got T.B and was taken away to a sanatorium in a dying state. I hardly saw her in my childhood. My father being a businessman had no time to attend to his children and I can never remember that he gave me even a shilling for pocket money. All the money I got, I had to earn by hard work and sweat. On the other hand, we always had enough to eat and he gave me a good education. I bear no hatred against him and I realized that he had his own troubles and worries and he tried his best according to his ability.

Whatever worries hurt you my child, please let me know. It does not matter if you criticize me because you will feel better and release the tension you have on your mind.

When I arrived, I found that Sylvia and you had left for Kenya. Did you get the money I sent you in Mengo? You both do the great mistake of writing at the last moment so it becomes impossible to arrange anything. Remember that it takes over ten days for a letter to reach me.

When I was last in Kampala, my wife and I visited Helene. She has a lovely baby boy. We both gave her presents.

Now remember my child I love and like you and I will do so always. Tell Sylvia that, too. Listen to me my child; I will never ever leave you as you say in your letter. But one thing you must do is never take council with your emotions and think that because other people go to the dogs you are apt to do the same. No! Think the best for yourself. Learn to adapt yourself to any

131

hardship in this world the best you know how. Learn to be grateful for whatever you have and make your life as you wish it to be, not a model of someone else's wrecked life. Be wise, kind and omniscient and eminently sensible, this is of immense help. There's no reason why you should not marry and be happy but for heaven sake get someone more reasonable, reliable and honest.

I hear over the radio that hell is let loose in Kampala and the Kabaka has disappeared. What a world we live in!

My profound love,
Daddy

This letter was the longest letter Daddy ever wrote; opening up about so many things I never knew. His mother was in a sanatorium since he was young. She died in 1951 of tuberculosis. His dear religious father Jakob brought up five children single-handedly. Jakob never remarried but continued working at his private business. Daddy, in a way, followed his father's footsteps as far as responsibility toward his children was concerned. Ulfhild had visited when politics turned haywire. Terrified, she rushed back to Norway. *No white foreigner was expelled at this time.*

Bjordal Mines Limited,
Kabale,
7th June 1966

Dear Mandy,

Many thanks for your letter of 27/5/66. Well I do not feel too bad as long as I take my tranquilizers, but I feel awful when I can't get them. I have had no news from the Doctor who was going to operate on me in Kampala but I hear he has just returned from leave, so no doubt I shall hear from him soon. Yes, everybody

132

has had this wretched flu followed with secondary infections such as tonsillitis, headaches and what have you. I have miraculously escaped it this year with only coughing and being deaf in one ear. I think it is going away slowly now. I hear a doctor in Kisoro is in critical condition at the moment.

You say Helene and George are the best couple in the world? Let us hope so.

The other day Helene asked to accompany me to Kabale. Why did I let her, I don't know. George was not happy. I advised her to comply with her husband and to be patient with him. It was just a Daddy's talk and I am glad she followed with good results in their relationship. A few days later, George walked around the house holding Helene like lovers do. I sent Sylvia money for her and Mother, chiefly for her to go to college and do typing.

We are doing quite well at present. In this fatal business, you need a good worker who supervises everything, has excellent organization skill, good memory and able to execute on the spar of moment. Problems are bound to happen haphazardly at mines. God help you if there is lack of capital.

Lots of love

Daddy.

I dreamt about running my own school. My Daddy would have been very proud and definitely helped me with the finances. Due to unavoidable circumstances, my dreams never materialized. Daddy became his own secretary as well as his own manager overworking himself even though doctors advised him to take easy. I asked him an unprofessional question about whether breathing of particles from heavy steel metallic elements might have made him sick. I had seen the fine, dusty Wolfram. He never wore a mask when working. *"Mining isn't the safest job on earth,"* I had said to him. Studying about psychological disturbances in children triggered my mind. Sylvia and I discussed this issue and thought we weren't quite normal. The truth was we were pretty normal happy girls. Both our homes provided plenty of love and attention. Mummy was within reach during the holidays and Daddy never discarded nor overlooked my many questions. Both parents fully interacted with us the best they knew how. To be very honest, I never saw my parents quarrelling or cursing or dissatisfied. I never imagined a man being mean to his wife or children. Later on in life, when I learnt about children suffering I was sicken to my soul and wished to open the biggest orphanage and take in suffering street children in my arms, my home and give them love. Opening up my feelings, I did not realize I'd hurt Daddy. On top of this he was dealing with Ulfhild mental illness. That is more problematic than other illnesses. I selfishly did not think what his sons went through either. I wished I were there to help Daddy with packing or something. I blessed wonderful Mserekano and Barnado for taking care of my Daddy. Sylvia and I took care of each other. Who was driving Daddy to the airport? I was sick with worries about what is going on in Uganda but was satisfied, in a way; Daddy would be away in Norway. Hope by then, the politics will be sorted out by the time he returns.

Bjordal Mines Limited,
Kabale, Uganda,
10ᵗʰ June 1966

Dearest Daughter

Many thanks for your greetings for my fifty one birthday on 4ᵗʰ of June. Nice of you to remember. You

134

are the only one who remembered it apart from Ulfhild. You should not worry about the politics in Uganda.

The only thing horrible is that Obote sent General Idi Amin to topple the King. Unfortunately Amin bombed and burnt the palace killing a lot of people. The royal family was arrested and some killed. I hope your mother and family are OK living so close to the palace.

Ulfhild and I were very lucky as we had been in Kampala hours before trouble started. That English fool, Dr. Parkinson, of a dentist made a mess of my teeth; it had gone to the roots. I had to remove my tooth.

Thanks for the photo; you look very smart and surprisingly healthy. Sylvia said she had lost her birth certificate when her bag was stolen. I have given her a scolding for carrying such a valuable document in her handbag which as you know is an object for sick pickpockets. Anyway, tell her I am not as angry as I made out to be.

I see you are having your teaching practice exam on 27th June and 22nd July. Hope you do your best and get good results. You are then assured of a good job later. Tell Sylvia to be sensible and finish her nursing certificates. Afterwards she can take up other things, such as being an airhostess.

Do not worry. Ulfhild does not read what I write to you or what you write to me. I ask her if she would want to write something.

With much love to you.
Daddy.

P.S. With regards to you from Ulfhild.

Reading Daddy's letter, I recall how Sylvia and I actually fell in love with this handsome dentist. Another

135

duplicate of Dr. Kildare, Richard Chamberlin. Boy he was good looking. For a fact, we looked for every possible excuse to have our teeth checked. He did, however, fill my molars. Being particular about the teeth, Daddy paid the bills without question. I was glad Daddy received his birthday card.

I had nightmares when the King's brother, Prince Henry visited me at college. You should have seen the members of staff peering behind curtains checking on me. Those taking a stroll whispered in each other's ears, suspiciously glancing at me as I hugged and kissed this prince. My Grandma and aunt had escaped safely to Kenya. Helene and Mother bravely stayed in troubled Uganda. I was sure glad Daddy would be safe up the mountain. *No evil gets up there.*

I never told Daddy I flew into trouble Uganda without a passport. It was like committing suicide. Being young and silly, I felt like a spy in the James Bond movies. I could not believe, timid me, locked up in a convent for eleven years, doing that. What was I thinking? Oh well, *It was great getting a free fare and pocket money. What an opportunity was that actually flying!* Watching James Bond movies was not a good thing.

Mr. Hayes, a journalist friend of Prince Henry, saw me off. As no news got out of Uganda, I was given details on how to record whatever I saw in cords, especially about the royal family. Being in a war zone, there is no time to write anything. If caught I'd disappear in Lake Victoria without a trace as many had done. My friend, *brain,* recorded everything to the minutest detail. Anyway, I was to bring his highness' passport secured at Mummy's home. Miss Hall listened on her extension and interrupted our plans. *You are not*

136

going anywhere Miss Bjordal. Your father has entrusted me with your wellbeing. Moreover you are about to sit for the final examinations!

"Miss Hall, were you are listening to my private conversation? I dare ask her. *I'm a college student now, you know.* "I am going for just one day." Miss Hall warned me if I was not back by Sunday she would telex my father. For a fact, she washed her hands of me in a letter that said, *"The college is not responsible for any mishap that might occur to Miss Margaret Bjordal once out of Nairobi."* Another said, *"Permission granted to Miss Margaret Bjordal to visit an ill grandma. She should return to Highridge Teacher's College by Sunday."*

I prayed so hard when flying with only tourists. The only brown persons in the plane were me and an Indian man. Deep inside of me, I suspected the passengers were journalists. What a wonderful unforgettable first experience I had in an aeroplane being enveloped in the clouds. The very clouds that Daddy and I had beneath our feet when I was little. But what a great risk I took!

Don't ask me how I missed both the check points in Nairobi and Uganda. As I was rushing out of a long queue at Entebbe someone shouted, *"Eh you!"* I stopped in my tracks thinking, *"This is it. I'm done."* Fortunately, someone else was being called back and I slipped in a white van with foreigners. We were stopped countless times along the twenty miles to Kampala by young boy-soldiers cocking their guns at our feet, dangling the rosary in my hands with the tip of the gun. Every couple of yards, there was a check point with jutting spikes on the road, inspected by underfed teenage soldiers dressed in camouflage, smoking awful cigarettes, *kali,* pointing AK rifles at our legs asking me

137

where my suitcase was. I said I only had hand luggage. *"Passport or papers?"* I produced my handwritten letter with a printed Highridge College address. It was looked at upside down and handed back to me. I remained calm.

After foreigners dispersed with friends to their destination, I was left alone at traveller's offices. Christ the King Church was padlocked so I continued my rosary outside asking Jesus for guidance.

A man in a battered taxi appeared and vowed he'd help me get home. As we passed through back roads I saw a few camouflaged soldiers. Kampala's seven hills had rising black clouds. Other than that, not a soul was around. I started a calm conversation in Luganda with the driver. Questioning someone is customary in Buganda. I was told many of his family had been tortured or killed. He seemed in favour of our overturned King Mutesa II, so I daringly said I was Princess Kajja Obunaku's Granddaughter. He got all excited and said he knew my family and took me directly home.

When I arrived not a sound was heard. After a while someone peeped by a curtain and said, *"Mandy!"* It was my mother. After the Buganda half hour greetings Mummy paid the driver and rushed me indoors. That night, older soldiers knocked at the door. Several entered and inspected the house for ammunitions and asked who I was as they had not seen me before. They were polite I must say. I slept fitfully as echoes of guns continued. In the dead of the night, dogs barked and there were indistinct cries of people clearly heard.

Next morning, with Prince Henry's passport secured in my pantyhose I walked alone to a bus stop near Bakuli market; not a soul was around. I continued praying. A handsome young foreigner stopped his car and offered me a lift. I thanked him as I got in. He asked me where my home was.

"I am not going home. I want to get to the Travel Agent opposite Christ the King church," I said thinking he was confused.

"I have to know where you live just in case we run into trouble," he said concernedly.

So I directed him home. Mummy was shocked and confused to see me back so soon with a white stranger. He walked into the house like he belonged there asking for the bedroom, for sex! Boy, did I let out whatever was on my mind as I stormed off with my luggage back to where I had started. Time was running short. I became panicky, nervous and really desperate. An Indian man, a shopkeeper, whom I recognized stopped. I didn't get into the car this time before interrogating him first. I outpoured my experiences a few minutes back. He said he knew my father and scolded me for being out in the streets. Anyway, we rushed and found the van about to leave with the same tourists, all silent. The driver said he specifically waited for me, expecting a tip. I thanked him, apologizing in Luganda that I did not have a penny in my name for a tip. I showed great gratitude. Can you imagine being stuck in a war zone city? If I got shot no one would have known.

I flew back to Nairobi storing what I had seen ready to give an account to my friends who thought I was crazy. *I could have given my poor Daddy a heart attack!* Anyway, I was happy I helped the family go to England, the country my Daddy praised so much. *Oh well, Daddy faced lions, leopards, rough rivers, the Sahara desert. I wanted to try it all. My uncle Sverre was a soldier at one time.*

Bjordal Mines Limited,
Kabale
15th June 1966

My dear Mandy,

Many thanks for your letter of 10th June. I wrote to you that you have to prove that you are Mandy instead of Margaret. I do not understand why the nuns did not accept your birth certificate name. I told you long ago that your therein name Mandy was misspelt as Mondy. No matter whether you like it I named you Mandy. Your mother insisted on Monday. When you receive your Teacher's Training Certificate you can say you falsified your name and show them your birth Certificate.

Do not worry about your exams. I shall write to the Principal, Miss Hall, and ask about your progress. I would like you to go abroad and will help you to do so after your exam. I am sure you will do no such thing as messing up your life.

I am enjoying the boys here. They have grown so tall. Braaken is now a head taller than me as well as Haakon. I shall take them to Queen Elizabeth's Park as I did first with you girls. I have been very ill lately, largely due to a virus attacking my breathing system, so I have difficulty breathing when sleeping at night.

What happened to Sylvia and her stolen passport? Forward me your birth certificate so I can see if I can get her another one.

Otherwise, I am not doing too badly at the mine and may be out of financial difficulties soon.

Love to Berit and Sylvia
Much love to you dear.
Daddy

PS Dear Mandy,

I don't think you have anything to worry about. You sound such a sensible girl. I hope you will come and spend part of your holidays here sometime. With best wishes, Ulfhild.

Wow. Ulfhild is sure nice. I thought.

My happy world came tumbling down. Instead of enjoying Independence as expected, fear slowly seethed into our very well being. Uganda was my country as Americans believe America is theirs. It's a beautiful thing to believe in belonging. Not only did I worry about my finals but the entire royal family. Where would Sylvia, Berit and I go when Uganda is in bloodshed; entirely alone in Kenya? Daddy seemed calm talking about his sons visit. Earlier on, in September 1966 I had asked Daddy why we never met our brothers. *Their mother never wanted them to.*

Bjordal Mines Limited,
Kabale, Uganda,
28th September 1966

My dear Mandy

Many thanks for your letter of 22nd September. Next time the boys come, you will definitely meet them.

So you want to study more at Kenyatta University? I thought you said you are tired of studies in one of your letters. Anyway, I'll do as you say as I know you are not wasting your time. What is as S1? If you want to become a writer or a poet you have to be really good in English. But you have a lot of talent. I've seen it in your paintings.

Everything is well at the mine. But Ulfhild is ill with the mysterious flu. She is ,as well, depressed. She sends her regards and best wishes to you. Sylvia   is   a sensible girl.   Tell her not to rush into marriage. There's plenty of time for all of you to choose your right man. Although marriage is a natural course for most humans; it can be dreadfully unpleasant and carries plenty of responsibilities, especially when children start coming. One has to be well equipped with experiences and knowledge about life before one starts on this difficult path.

With lots of love to you and Sylvia,

Daddy

Daddy seemed to have another worry about Sylvia as I did. Sylvia fell in love with an English man. Nairobi Hospital was still predominately white or English. On visiting her, I met a divorced young man at the dance, full of woes practically crying for his ex-wife. Yet he talked about taking me to bed. The *outside* world is sure weird just as the nuns had warned us.   I wanted to further my teaching career at Kenyatta University for a secondary teacher's degree; mainly I'd earn more money. They were offering scholarships. But I was determined to fend for myself soon.

Bjordal Mine Limited,
Kabale,
10th October 1966.

My dearest Mandy,

You are right. I'm glad you were able to handle him. To answer your question, NO, it is not right to kiss or fondle a girl at the first dance, for heaven sake. Do not worry Mandy you are very normal. You should have told the guy he did not have any grey matters. That would have made him think. Keep away from men who

142

drink. I have always HATED that. As long as you do not bring yourself to their level and very diplomatically hold your esteem, you will be respected. I am happy however that you are going out dancing. I know how you girls love that and are terrific dancers.

Again you are wise to keep away from recently divorced guys. They are usually not quite over their aches and may just want your comfort.

Try and find out how Sylvia feels about such things. Does she just fall in love with anyone who shows her love? She is pretty young to get serious with anyone at the moment. Politics don't seem very safe here in anymore. You will have to be careful when you come home.

There is a lot of disagreement with the Royal Dynasty and the Common Man's Charter. Prime Minister Obote wants to do away with royal family which Britain is supportive; like they don't have royalties in England. Even Norway has it.

Lots of love to both of you,

Daddy.

Sylvia forgot how Daddy cautioned us about rushing into marriage. *Always take your time. Learn the man thoroughly.* Daddy never admitted his hurtful experiences. All his women had been ten or fifteen years younger than him. Women his age were married with children. He was a good man, my Daddy was. No one could shake a finger at me and tell me otherwise. Daddy warned me about the instability of politics in Uganda. We had lived in peace from time memorial.

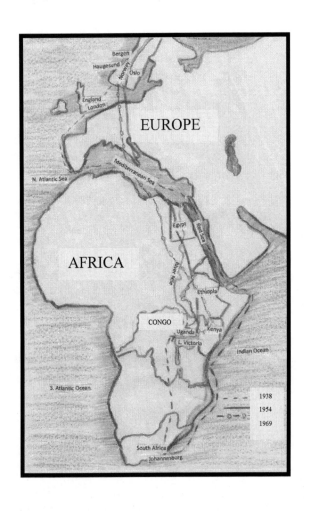

Daddy's Journeys 1938-1969

CHAPTER SEVEN
TOO MANY CHANGES

Bjordal Mines Limited
Kabale, Uganda.
10th January 1967

My dear Mandy,
I received your letter of 4th January. Thank you very much. I am glad Sylvia is taking swimming. You never tried that after your nearly drowning experience in 1962, have you? Sylvia mentioned taking up private music as well. Good for her. What happened to your music? You said you would take it up after school. You had done pretty well in the first four grades and had only two left to qualify. Anyway, think about it.

Sylvia is learning to control her emotions. This is indeed a step forward in life. I want you as big sister to encourage her to get a good grip of the nursing career. I still wish she will fulfill her dream of being an air-hostess.

Lots of love,
Daddy

The 'boys' were doing pretty well in school and had grown a head taller than him showing us photos of them. Haakon had grown his hair *like the Beatles.* Daddy's elder brother had a stroke and was bedridden. I knew very little about his immediate family and asked about that part of him.

His father, Jakob Bjordal, was born in 1886 and his mother in 1885. *That was when my Great grandfather, King Mwanga ll persecuted and killed young Catholic and Protestant believers.*

145

Daddy's elder brother, Torman was born in 1911, his older sister Aaslaug was born 1913. Uncle Henrick Sverre was born 1917 and his youngest sister, Birgit was born 1921. I had forgotten their names. Luckily, my second cousin Nina sent me Daddy's family history. I knew for sure his father was named Jakob. Mummy has only one sister and a brother who died when young.

Sylvia came to the college with a new boyfriend and we went to an English club at Karen for swimming. I do not swim. The young man looked like what Daddy might have called *a vagabond!* That too, was my unfortunate judgment. Whilst we were swimming, he disappeared and we had to take a taxi back to Nairobi.

Although I was pretty happy and normal I began to think otherwise. Sylvia and I planned to question Daddy in our next letters. I had been taking a *Child Psychology* course and had started to question our upbringing.

> *Bjordal Mines Limited,*
> *Kabale,*
> *29th February 1967*

Dear Mandy,

I was so shocked with your letter and wished I was dead. I did not expect this after all the years I tried taking care of you. You were the apple in my eye. I had hoped you would turn out into something instead of sitting there blaming someone's mistakes to your unhappiness. You know what Mandy? As from now on I wash my hands off you. Do what you can for yourself.

> *Daddy*

When Sylvia and I met I asked her if Daddy wrote to her. She said yes he did. He wrote a nice letter to her. She casually said she did not write what we had planned. My letter was filed! How could I hurt Daddy? I sent him an Easter card with the following message:

My dearest Daddy,

I am so sorry,

Your prodigal daughter,

Mandy

I believed that was the end of Daddy and me. But he immediately wrote back to me.

Bjordal Mines limited,
Kabale,
28th March 1967.

My dear Daughter,

I thank for your Easter signed 'Prodigal Daughter" which means recklessly wasteful'. I don't think that is a right title for you. You were once thoughtless but not prodigal. Anyway I got over the shock of what you wrote to me, slowly. The best we can do is to forget about it altogether. I, on my part as your father, would like to see that you are fairly happy in life and I hope no one is going to hurt you. And you on your part should understand it is not easy as you think to be as good a father as you are building up in your mind. Many parents don't come up to the expectations of their children. I always did my best for you, Mandy, in particular so this is why I did not believe my eyes when I read your letter. It hurt me so much I wished I had never been born, especially coming from you Mandy. Think of the millions of children in this world who don't even get food, education, and clothing. When your mother took you from me, the court said to pay her thirty shillings per child that was all. But I could not

147

live with myself without visiting you, bringing you food and educating you.

Anyway, I am interested to know what you are doing back in Maryhill. Are you employed as a teacher there?

I am not well at all Mandy, and might go to Europe at the beginning of May. If I can find a way to get off from this God damned place where there is nothing but work and worries that should help. Ulfhild said she will take care of the mine with the help of the German manager. I have to lie in hospital for most of the time, I suppose.

With much love from your,
Daddy

I honestly did not mean to hurt him. I told him, regrettably, that he did not care for us. That he had no idea what it was not having your parents around. I selfishly forgot about my Australian brother who never met his father or my Norwegian brothers who only saw him a couple of times since they moved to Norway in 1963. I should have known better. Unfortunately our letters crossed. After reading his letter, I wished I were home to apologize and hug him and cry on his shoulders. I could not handle so many changes in my life at this period.

As soon as I posted Daddy my letter, I received one from him informing me about his heart condition. I regretted sending him that letter and there was nowhere reversing what I had written. I still comforted myself that he would live to a ripe age. Daddy was only fifty-one years old. Every time Daddy left for Norway I thought I'd never see him again. Just a month later, we were back to being friends.

Bjordal Mines Limited,

148

Kabale, Uganda
June 1967

My dear Daughter,

I'm leaving for Norway. I have asked Ulfhild to help you and Sylvia get your passports. You have to get two passport photographs. I shall see what doctors can do for me in Norway. I hope all will go well with you in my absence.

Lots of love,
Daddy

This short letter came a whole six weeks before my class examinations. I had reports to complete and to pack up before the end of July. I was in Uganda the beginning of August. Then, of course, there were the arrangements to meet Ulfhild. Without the access of a telephone it was another story. We could have sent a telegram but that too took forever to reach Kabale.

Bjordal Mines Limited
Kabale,
25th June 1967

Dear Mandy,

I have been to Kampala to fetch your passports as they refused to send them by post to Kenya or anywhere else. So please, let me know when you will be in Kampala next so that I can hand them over to you personally. The same applies to Sylvia's passport, but that you can carry with you when you go back to Kenya.

I have had a letter from Harald. He is now finished with the examinations in hospital in Norway and has been told he has a damaged heart and will live on salt free food diet and live the life of a semi-invalid for the rest of his remaining life. That is a big blow on both of

149

us, as he will be unable to do much work anymore, and I don't know how we are going to manage.

Please don't delay in letting me know when you arrive in Kampala as it is difficult for me to get away on short notice.

When you see Sylvia, please give her my salaams.

Has Berit started moving with her passport? For God sake, tell her to start moving with getting the forms I gave you and the photos needed and send them to me, she must not wait until somebody does it for her. It is getting more and more difficult getting a passport as time goes by.

Your

I received an unsigned, explicit letter from Ulfhild but I did not complain as Daddy did for my unsigned letters.

Daddy had left that June and I had not heard from him, therefore was worried sick. Having met Ulfhild and Berit I thought they had accepted me as family and would inform me if Daddy was gravely ill. I was Bjordal's daughter after all. I wrote to my niece, Berit, inquiring whether Daddy was dying, threating that I'd go to the Norwegian Embassy in Kenya and find out about my Daddy if I heard nothing in two weeks' time.

I got a letter from Berit sooner than expected. She said Daddy did not give her instructions to tell me anything. At the same time, she sent my letter to Daddy.

Bjordal Mines Limited,
10th August 1967

Dear Mandy,

I am back from Norway. Ulfhild gave me the letter you had written her. First of all I'm not dying. I am only tired and a bit sick. But now I'm fifty two years old

150

and my poor heart is getting old and tired. I shall have to take it easy both physically and psychologically.

I am glad you had a nice time at the coast with your college friends. This makes me feel much better. I want you to be happy remember that.

I would advise you girls, as a father, not to rush into marriage; I hope you will take me seriously. I want you to work and have some savings to fall back to just in case something drastic happens with the marriage. I'm not discouraging you but I want you to be prepared of unforeseen circumstances

Ulfhild informed me that your passports were ready but you and Sylvia were so irresponsible and careless. You did not keep in touch and you gave her headaches because you do not follow her instructions. She could not send them through the post as it is against the law; they have to be handed to you by hand. Another thing you are issued travelling papers. These are very important documents. These must be handed over to the Principle Immigration Officer in Kampala on your return to Uganda. PLEASE DO NOT FORGET!

Hearing this about the two of you, who have always been hardworking and trustworthy and have never bothered me with even asking for money, I am very disappointed and still getting over it.

You disturbed her so much that she is going back to Norway in September. As it is, she was near a nervous breakdown when the German manager was cut in the head and speared through the knee. However, he managed to kill one attacker and cut another.

All this happened whilst I was in Europe. I shall now work by myself for four months. I don't know how I

151

shall manage as the doctors said to take it easy. Anyway, I hope I'll be O.K.

Please give my love to the other girls. No matter what I shall always love you.

Yours sincerely,

Daddy

How could Ulfhild do that to a sick man? I could not believe reading about the problems we gave her. Sylvia and I were there at the appointed building as expected. Ulfhild seemed happy to see us and introduced us to an extremely tall African lawyer. Princess Bagaya, the first African woman lawyer in East Africa, reigned magisterial beauty as swiftly passed us. Ulfhild stood in her tracks and commented on her beauty, height, figure and particularly the long hair she had. We casually told Ulfhild her sister studied with us at Maryhill.

Papers were signed and we went over to the Government passport department causing quite a spectacular amongst many white people. There we were a white woman, an African man and two beige girls. Realizing the awkwardness, Ulfhild reintroduced us to the lawyer making sure the crowd understood we had no connections with her. *We did not shake hands as told as we already done so at our first introduction.* How ridiculous was that? Sylvia was dying with laughter. I believe Ulfhild sent our passport to Nairobi. Daddy forgot he had already given me the news of the drama at the mine but I studied the letter and found a little more caption added. Although I never took Ulfhild mental illness seriously now I understood she was a very disturbed woman. Mummy was aware of it but never said a word.

Everything went upside down at the mine during his absence.

Luckily, the German manager saved himself using a slashing knife; killing one of the thugs.

Sylvia as well decided to get married at this point so I rushed back to Nairobi only to find that she had broken off the wedding and had given back the engagement ring to her fiancé. I unexpectedly landed at Sylvia's friend's house at Hurlingham. Her English father boomed that his daughter had no right picking up someone from the streets. I wished the earth-would-open-up and-swallow me. The nuns had put the fear of sin sleeping at a hotel otherwise I'd have gone there. I shared a bed with Sylvia and was awake the whole night worried the matron might find me. Early next morning, I slipped out of the Nurses' Mess and took a bus to Eastleigh to my dear Ethiopian friend.

Bjordal Mines Limited,
Kabale, Uganda,
17ᵗʰ September 1967

My dear Daughter,

Many thanks for your two letters; one from Thika and one from Mombasa. I am glad you enjoyed Mombasa.

The (boys) servants carried the dying German man to our house. Can you imagine carrying an unconscious man up a steep hill in pitch-black night? Even you young girls laboured up breathlessly. Can you imagine my wife's state of mind when she saw the blood-covered man? She rushed and drove him to hospital; fortunately he recovered.

The manager did not take care of the mine properly when I was away in Norway. I was to find out that one by one the machineries had broken.

153

You ask if I enjoyed Europe. I did not enjoy it at all due to the awful weather which is too cold and too wet. However, I enjoyed seeing my boys again.

Mombasa is a good place for a holiday. That's where I met my Australian wife. The biggest mistake I ever made. This is why I tell you girls not to rush into marriage.

Anyway, it was good to be in Europe, getting away from that deadly work for two years without a break. It did me good despite the bad weather.

I now sleep well at night, a thing I couldn't do before I just stayed awake worrying.

With much love,

Daddy

I was at peace hearing Daddy was happy to find his sons had grown so much taller than him. I smiled when he complained about the European weather. *You were born in it;* I wanted to say to him. My Daddy loved Africa. Daddy sure did appreciate being away from work and endless worries, happily visiting family. I never asked him whom did my brothers stay with when their mother visited Daddy? Were they at a boarding school? Why did Ulfhild not bring them over when she visited Daddy?

Bjordal Mines Limited,
Kabale
21st October 1967

My dear Mandy,

Many thanks for your letter of 16th October. Helene told me that Sylvia had a nervous breakdown after breaking off with her boyfriend and had to see a psychiatrist. Is that true? I do hope the poor girl is over it now and is much wiser.

154

We all have these tragic love affairs in our youth. I have had mine. It's painful, but once you are over it one becomes stronger and mature. Who knows, she may have been lucky beyond her imagination.

When I was in Norway last summer, I met the woman who broke my heart. I have never seen such an ugly being. For a moment, I thought I must be mistaken. But there she was my 'childhood dream' with grey, flossy hair, wrinkles all over, no teeth and fat like a pig and a heavy drinker. I went away counting my blessings.

Please get me Sylvia's address. My love to Berit.
So long and hope to see you and Mary.

Daddy

A whole term went on peacefully. Sylvia was back to her jovial self. I told my adventurous Maltese friend about Daddy. She said she'd love to meet him and perhaps have some of the adventures I spoke about. *More than any of my sisters I brought the most friends to the mine.*

Bjordal Mines Limited
Kabale,
28th November 1967

My dearest Mandy,

I am sorry I cannot pick you up due to pressing situation. I am sure you and your friend Mary could take a bus and come over. Let me know the date and I will pick you at Kabale. I am trying to settle everything before you arrive so we can have some time together. I may visit some of the mines so it will be fun to have some company on these tedious journeys.
I am looking forward to meeting your Maltese friend.

See you soon,
Daddy

Sister Anastasia unexpectedly asked me to take along an orphan girl. Both her parents were alive but for some reason the nuns had adopted her. I wrote to Daddy everything about her: she was half-caste with blonder hair, bluer-eyes than him and a horribly pale skin.

My Maltese friend, Mary Brincat, insisted on hitchhiking. At one point, after being dropped at a *God-forsaken-place,* as Daddy often said; we walked mile after mile with not a car or human in sight; just dried balls of leaves harried by the wind passed us. Priscilla, the poor girl almost fainted from exhaustion and being parched. However, we finally managed a country bus to Kabale. On arrival some individuals exclaimed how I looked like my father. I was proud to resemble the handsomest man in the world. I accidently bumped into my Norwegian cousin, Berit, and she took us to the German manager staying at a guest house. The manager had been ill with a bout of flu.

"I might as well take you to your father and get back to work," he said reluctantly.

When I met Daddy tears pooled in his eyes saying, *"I am not even blessed to have my children here with me."* I deeply felt his loneliness. I was beyond emotions or affection to cry too instead I hugged him tightly. I saw only the warmth and loving affectionate side of Daddy.

What a memorable holiday, Daddy gave me and my friends. In the evening after dinner and a chat, we went to bed quite exhausted. Working tediously the whole day I had hoped he'd relax in bed; reading with glasses perched on his nose instead.

One evening, I walked up to the office and asked Daddy if he minded my company. He placed the pen down, smiled inviting me in and pointed at a seat. Not being business minded I asked to have a look at photographs bursting in envelopes on the shelf. "*Oh sure, sure,*" he said. I came across a pretty European woman asking if she was his sister. I had never seen that black and white photo before. There were plenty of Ulfhild. Surpringly a few of her in the depths of the forest swimming nude.

"*Well, that is Marjory, my Australian ex-wife,*" he said.

"Wow, you had another wife before Ulfhild?" I asked. None of us knew of Marjory. I am sure neither did his Norwegian sons.

"*Well we met in Mombasa and married shortly. About three week or three months I can't remember which,*" he said.

"How did you meet an Australian out there in Mombasa? And Daddy began this story.

In nineteen-fifty, after your Mother took you away I had to have a holiday. I went to a European club in Mombasa to socialize and there I met this incredibly beautiful cabaret dancer, Marjory. She was visiting friends in Mombasa from Pemba. Within a few days, we married at an Anglican Cathedral with mainly Europeans present January of 1950. She was a smart outgoing woman.

We drove from Mombasa to Nairobi right through rough roads with wild animals everywhere. Mombasa and Pemba at this time had mainly Arabs, Asians and plenty of Europeans and English sailors besides indigenous Africans.

Terrified, Marjory cried all the way to Nairobi. Not only was she afraid of wild animals but of Africans. To make matters worse, Africans rather enjoyed
157

*frightening white people. When I was not sure where I was going, I'd ask for help. Bwana, they would say, there is a stampede of elephants approaching and they run off giggling. Marjory thought we'd be stampeded. Kenya had thousands upon thousands of elephants and wild animals everywhere. It was nothing like today. Marjory loved the exotic life in Pemba and Mombasa due to civilization found on those Islands. When we landed here in the bundu (**bush**), she clung on me for dear life also when she saw half naked people. Marjory must have had cultural shock, unlike me who has seen thousand naked people from south of Egypt, the Sudan, and Kenya and of course right here in Kabale.*

I must say Marjory loved the mine, although she criticized me for having unqualified workers. I trained them for God sakes. I treated her like a queen with six servant ready at her service. As you know, I am hapless with the kitchen, ironing and housework. When I came home from work exhausted beyond words, they carried hot water from the kitchen below to the tub. You know how things run here. Unlike colonialists who called their servants 'boy', I called mine by their names; Mserekano and Barnado. I had a nanny to take care of you as well when my brother, Sverre, brought you back.

Coming from warm Australia Marjory found mountainous Kigezi very cold. Had I known how miserable she'd be I'd never have married her. Her tears and whining drove me crazy and I packed her back to Australia and supported her. Exactly nine months later I had a letter that she had a baby named Raymond, born October of 1950 and christened at St Augustine Church, in Australia. Wow, my sister Berit was born March the same year!

"What do you think Mandy? Does Raymond look anything like me?" he asked me showing me the photograph.

"How old is he?" I asked.

"He has just turned seventeen years in October."

"Wow, Daddy, you have children with three different women?" I asked without thinking.

"This why you girls feel I am strict. I do not want you to make the same mistakes, I have made with my life. Marjory had hoped I'd leave Africa and join them in Australia. And do what there? I'd have missed seeing you grow up, the business that I have built. I had no idea, she was with child in just three weeks? Even if we are apart now, at least, I am able to visit you in Mengo." Speaking with such warmth and eloquence, I believed him. I was dying to ask Daddy why he never invited us for holidays all these years restarting only after Ulfhild left but was careful not to churn up unpleasant topics as I did in 1967.

Daddy surprised me with questions about Romeo with a transfixed severity, his voice a deep drawl. That is exactly what he said to Sylvia two years earlier.

It was on an evening as we sat at the veranda, the moon above shimmering; his light blue eyes seem to reflect the very same clouds as they did when I was a little child. I wished Romeo were here to experience these panoramic views. Knowing Daddy believed in frankness rather than deceptiveness, I answered his questions to the best of my ability, *short but precise.*

Is he serious? Probably. *Is he responsible*? He seems to be. *Is he a womanizer*? Not that I know of. *Does he drink*? Only at dances. Romeo has whisky on the rocks and I enjoy gin and lime. *Is he trustworthy?* Maybe. I promised Daddy to drop Romeo like hot coal

159

if he was not. Daddy smiled as if saying, that's *my girl*. Daddy felt responsible for our final jump in life trusting we were secure, comfortable and most importantly happy. I can hear, *In My Father's House,* by Elvis Presley as I write.

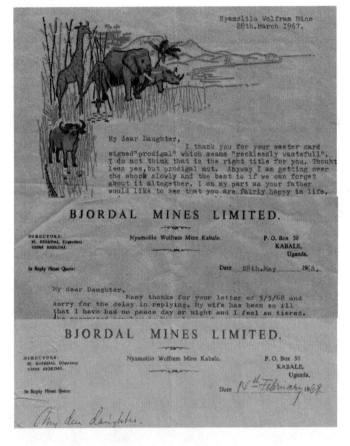

Letters from Daddy, handwritten ones are my favourite

CHAPTER EIGHT
LAST PREPARATIONS

Daddy seemed like he was going somewhere; packing up, organizing our passports, denying his Norwegian citizenship and becoming Ugandan, advising me to open a bank account and saving.

Directors; Harald Bjordal (Ugandan)
Ulfhild (Norwegian)

> Bjordal Mines Limited,
> Kabale,
> 27th January 1968.

My dear Mandy,

I am glad you received the passports although it's illegal to send them by post. Ulfhild did it anyway! She could easily have dropped them at your mother's even if she did not get out of the car.

Do not be disturbed if you do not hear from me. Sometimes as many as ten uninvited government officials turn up at my house sleeping here like in a hotel. What am I to do? I can't tell them not to come in or that I am not well. Who believes I'm sick except you. I am so sick Mandy with not a soul around.

I have renounced my Norwegian citizenship after 53 years. When I got my Uganda passport my photograph was fine but the information was hilarious. It was written Mr. Patel--, eyes and hair black. Even with a black and white photograph you can see my light eyes and light hair.

How's my dear Sylvia getting on? Before Ulfhild left she met (I will not mention the name) told her that

161

you girls said I do not help you in anyway? How about that! Is that true?

With kind regards,
Daddy

What I loved about Daddy was that he never believed in hearsay from anyone but in what *we* actually said. He was frank: he never beat around the bush. He called *a spade a spade,* hoping we would be likewise.

Becoming a Ugandan citizen after all these years, definitely proved he wasn't going back to Norway no matter how bad the political situation was.

I had a relaxing holiday with my Indian friends at the coast, wishing Daddy had come for a little rest. Sea level is good for people with high blood pressure.

My Maltese friend left for Malta, her position was replaced by a very beautiful French lady ten years my senior. She looked way younger than me. As we shared the house, I had hoped to polish my French but she was determined to learn English from me.

Bjordal Mines Limited,
Kabale, Uganda,
2ⁿᵈ March 1968

My dear Mandy,

Thanks a lot for your letter. I am awfully sorry I did not come to see you off at the station or earlier. As you know Ulfhild arrived from Europe. No sooner had she done so when she went down with a severe attack of flu and asthma. Up to date, she has not recovered. She seems at least to be feeling better. I have been so worried and unhappy because of this. On the 10ᵗʰ March, I shall take her to Kampala for a checkup again!

So you met Mr. Lien at the station when you left? That was nice. About your cousin, Berit's address, I think if you write to the Matre Norwegian International Voluntary Service and Rehabilitation Centre in Mbarara; she will get your letter.

I am glad you and Sylvia will see each other again. Give her my love. I see Berit is not getting much of a salary. When I was young I got 30 shillings to begin with. She also can start at the bottom, get experience, slowly build herself up and get a better salary.

> *I hope you are well dear.*
> *With love,*
> *Daddy*

My main reason for wanting my cousin Berit's address was to become closer. We never addressed each other as cousins. Daddy wrote about his niece not my cousin. We had a very short weekend at the mine and the Salt Lake and she was shocked to see me tan so quickly. In just a day, my skin peeled.

By this time, many friends helped me pray for my Daddy. How do you cope with a damaged heart? People with flu and mental health issues usually cope pretty well with medication. I did not have much to say to Daddy except that I was praying for him.

> *Bjordal Mine Limited,*
> *Kabale, Uganda,*
> *12th March 1968*

My dear Daughter,

Thanks for your letter of 10/3/68. I am sorry I have been unable to reply earlier. Ulfhild's asthma kept me awake now a whole month as she is getting worse. She is at the moment in Kabale hospital, staying with the Sister in charge there. I can now sleep well, but am still

163

worried about her health. I think she is invaded with some strange viruses.

Like Sylvia was, Ulfhild is ever depressed, bordering nervous breakdown. But she will get better, I am sure of that. I am not feeling too bad myself at present although I did get some of those asthma symptoms. How did you as a child cope with it and your aching bones without complaining leaves me to wonder? But you let me hypnotize you when little. Remember that? Ulfhild won't let me do it on her.   I must congratulate you for your raise in payment. As I say this wretched taxation take an enormous bite out of your earnings. That is for sure.

I have seen that here at the mine how profit is dwindling year by year. The latest stunt is something called 'Pension Fund' whereby the workers' pay 5% on their wages and the employer pays another 5%. I have over three hundred employees to pay and 1500 shillings more. This I cannot afford and may have to close down the mine. These people go from one extreme to another, killing the goose that lays the golden egg. Of course that money will find a way to the privilege people's pockets, as always.

We are having some curious rain up at Kigezi at present which seem to penetrate the roads to such an extent that traffic churn the roads up to seas of mud and traffic comes to a standstill. The road to Kampala has been blocked several times this month.

I am pleased that you have a new room at the school you are teaching at and that you keep it spotlessly clean. This habit will benefit you in life. People will notice and respect you.

Sylvia wrote that Berit was accepted at Teacher's college in Meru, Kenya; that is good news. She was working for the Epaminondas. Helene is now in Mbale.

Well my dear this is for now,

With much love

Dad

I learnt something interesting about Norwegians. If siblings had a daughter they had the same name. I have two cousins and a sister called Berit. At that time Daddy said the Bjordal name belonged to one family. That it would be easy to find my uncles, nephews or cousins in Bergen or Haugesund. Now the name Bjordal or Harald are in thousands.

I loved the way Daddy kept me in touch about my sisters as they were not keen in writing letters as Daddy and I were. My sister Berit got herself into college entirely on her own. Meru is very far from Thika. My Maltese friend, Mary Brincat, and I hitchhiked to Meru and surprised Berit with our visit. She was living at an Italian nuns' community. We stayed at *Pig and Whistle* hotel and had dinner. Hearing outrageously loud music of the Kenya Army Band, we were excited there was dancing going on. Unfortunately, it was an army dance with very few ladies. Being, assumingly, the only *foreigners,* every soldier wanted to dance with us. I never told Daddy this. To know I was surrounded by so many men he would have had a fit. The smell of beer and rowdiness made us leave earlier than expected. Next morning we hitchhiked back to Thika after seeing Berit, Meru town and the snowcapped Mt. Kenya. We had all sorts of lifts including an army man. He tested us with a question, " *What if I divert into the bush?"* My heart skipped a beat and boldly said I'd jump out of

165

car. I'd rather die than be touched. He assured us he'd drop us at the designated place.

The most remembered transport was from an English farmer in a van full of Alsatians. He stopped and angrily shouted, *"Get in the bloody car! What are foreign girls doing out here in the middle of wilds. Do you have any bloody idea you are walking within a park?"* It was the worst lift I ever had with so much cursing, the dogs' heavy panting with drools and foam at their mouths, some even landed on our blouses. I was never as terrified as that day.

It was soon Sylvia's twenty first birthday on the 31st of March. She had a small party at our Ethiopian friend's house then went dancing at a club. The music and all the fast dancing were great. Slow dances were for the old people if you saw any in clubs. Daddy would have found this place madness. He loved slow, soft music most time.

Bjordal Mines Limited,
Kabale,
4th April 1968

Dear Daughter,

Many thanks for your letter of 24/3/68. I note that you are coming down to Kampala, but you do not say what date. Please let me know immediately when you and Sylvia are coming so I can be in Kampala to fetch you. Looks like you had some adventure going to Meru. Be careful, Mandy. Hitch-hiking on deserted roads alone is not safe. This is why I will personally pick you from Kampala instead of letting you find your way up the mine.

Ulfhild is still sick in Kampala and apart from asthma she is suffering from Spondylitis, a type of arthritis down her neck and arm.

166

My niece Berit from Mbarara is coming for Easter. I have to go fetch her at Kabale on the 16th April.

I am sorry Mandy, this is just a hurried letter in order to inform you what is going on here. I do hope I am lucky to see you both in Kampala. I leave the mine on the 7th (Sunday) and will probably return on the 13th April.

Lots of love to you both,
Daddy

We nervously spent our holiday with Ulfhild even though she was surprisingly friendly. She did not seem as sick as I had imagined. I had tons of questions to ask her but I sealed my mouth as Mummy had cautioned me to. Daddy had taught me not to be afraid of asking questions. I battled with both contradictions, *" Feel free to ask, don't you dare ask."*

What a quiet, boring holiday that was. Daddy left in the morning and was back in the evenings: no more adventurous trips to the forests, no more sitting together having debates, and no more dancing to Straus. Tea was brought by the servant on the verandah to Ulfhild as she sat in an armchair; her feet rested upon a cushioned stool reading. Sylvia and I trimmed off dried leaves from Daddy's flower garden. Ulfhild invited us over to tea and we had cryptic conversations. I was dying to hear something about Haakon and Braaken. Instead she said, "Tomorrow we will go shopping at Kabale for new clothes!" Wow! Ulfhild was to buy us readymade clothes. Disappointedly; we went to an Indian shop and bought one and half yard piece of material each! Ulfhild insisted Sylvia buy a light pink material pointing out she was fairer and I a dark maroon because I was darker. Differences in colour was never pointed to us; Mummy always dressed us alike. We both preferred

167

each other's material. Ulfhild bought a paper pattern to cut a dress and we hand stitched under supervision. Little did Ulfhild know we were experts in dress making on a Singer Sewing Machine. Both Mummy and the school taught us stitching. The dresses were literally straight like a sack.

> *Bjordal Mine Limited,*
> *Kabale, Uganda,*
> *28th May 1968*

My dear Daughter,

Many thanks for your letter of 5/5/68 and sorry for the delay in replying. Ulfhild has been so ill that I have had no peace day and night and I feel so tired.

She recovered in Kampala so she thought of joining me back to Kigezi. As soon as she comes here she feels sick again. At present, she is staying with a doctor at Kabale.

What is it going to be like when the boys come from Norway I do not know, but I suppose I will manage?

You asked about the mine. Well, my dear, everything is O.K; the price has fallen on the world market and it is difficult to make it pay just now. I met my niece Berit at Mbarara and she sent her love to you. She has not been well either. We all have our problems, have we not, Mandy? I have given money to your mother to fix something about the house; do not mention it in your letter. Otherwise, Ulfhild gets angry. What I'm doing is for you girls.

Ulfhild is suffering from a nervous breakdown at present and magnifies small happenings to the extreme. I shall send her to Europe for a few years. The attack on the German manager precipitated the breakdown. I have no manager but I find I can manage better on my own. Demitrius will be coming from Tanzania; I have

168

no choice but to take him back although I do not trust him as I used to.

My Berit has left working for Costas and is going for a job as children's nurse at Namirembe.

Give my love to Sylvia and thank her for the letter she sent.

With love

Daddy

I felt sorry for Daddy. Besides the responsibility of the mine, he had a patient to care for. Even if I offered my help, he would not have accepted it. With plenty of teachers in Kenya, I could have afforded taking time off work. Daddy openly told me how sick he was. From nineteen sixty-three to now he practically lived alone. I wondered what that was like going home in solicitude accompanied with howling winds and rumbling thunder. I comforted myself that he had happy days as a young man travelling as a sailor, the fun he had in South Africa and Mombasa and the gratification he had when he became a wealthy man in the fifties.

There was no letter from Daddy for a whole month and I became concerned.

Nyamolilo Mines Limited,
Kabale
5th July 1968.

My Dear Daughter,

I am so sorry I have not been able to write to you sooner. I have had so many problems to tackle that it has made me sick. First of all, Ulfhild fell sick upon me and had to be taken to a mental hospital called Butabika, outside Kampala. Then our sons arrived from Europe and I have to take care of them on my own.

The machinery on the mine broke as well to top my problems that I tackle on my own.

169

Well this is all very depressing news so let's talk of something more cheerful. Haakon and Braaken just love it here in Africa. They are both taller than me. I was supposed to take them to the park but due to pressing work I have been unable to.

When I was last in Kampala I saw your mother and Berit and they sent their love to you. I was supposed to take the Haakon and Braaken to meet their sisters but I fell ill. When I felt a little better I rushed back to the mine.

I am sorry to hear you had asthma as well. Ulfhild is sick with one ailment or another and I will send her back with the boys.

Many thanks for your good wishes for my fifty three birthday. You advised me to take it easy, but it looks like I get more and more work as time goes on. It is impossible to get anyone to take over the work. That means I will have to do it on my own. The German man was not too bad at the beginning but he neglected the machines when I was in Europe.

As for your flu, use Milton and gurgle everyday twice a day. That's how eventually I get rid of mine.

I had a letter from Sylvia. I hope she will come up here for her holidays.

This is for all now, my dear. I have to rush down to the mine in order to see if I can fix the engines.

All the best to you and lots of love.

Daddy

I was sorry I did not see Daddy this time as I did not want to get in the way between him and Ulfhild even though he said she was OK with us. I had my doubts. If she was OK wouldn't we have gone on holidays at least once a year our entire life? I was really surprised that Daddy wanted to finally introduce us to

170

our brothers. Was it his final wish? It certainly was. Did they at least know of us the past years? I never found out. We knew of them since birth.

I had been ill with bronchitis. Even the English doctor gave up on me and rudely told me, " *Leave my office and make yourself better!* " Wow. What is wrong with people or is it my karma? I managed with asthma pretty well but bronchitis is even more painful. I missed two weeks of work. Sister Anastasia walked up to my room telling me I had taken much too time off work. I dressed and went coughing to work.

> *Nyamolilo Mines Limited,*
> *Kabale, Uganda,*
> *30th July 1968*

My dear Mandy,

Thanks for your letter with no date. I am afraid even my letter is late. As you know, the boys are still here. We have just come home from a hunting Safari near Queen Elizabeth's Park. They are both mad about hunting and I had to take them for a game treat. Considering the fact that they never even touched a big gun, they were quite good.

One of them hit a Topi and the other a Uganda Cob. They shot a guinea fowl and a partridge and did quite well. It was quite tough on me now that I am getting old but it was fun for them all the same.

We drove around the park right up to Kabatoro and stayed in a hotel. The whole village was deserted as you know there are problems in Uganda. Mr. Youtoglou was not there even, so we cooked our own food. We returned after three days completely exhausted. The boys love it here in Africa and they got a nice tan almost your colour. I am sorry to hear you got bronchitis. Does the school not give you a health

171

insurance? I honestly do not understand the insensitivity of that nun. It's beyond me. Drink plenty of hot lemon and honey that is sure to help you. I am proud your class did such a lovely display in art and you were so praised. I always said you were gifted in art. If you meet Mzee Jomo Kenyatta, tell him you come from a good family in Norway and that your family in Uganda is royal. A very good mix.   My wife has been surprisingly fine and is going back with the sons on 14th August. I'm sorry I forgot your birthday on 6th of August. You know I remembered you in my heart but due to all the excitement I did not have the time to send you a card. I'm sorry. I shall once again be on my own, a fact that I do not look forward to. I am not feeling too bad at present, but there is some serious malfunction in my coronary circulation and am going to be admitted in Mulago sometime this month .   My niece said you had a nice figure and were beautiful. She was here with her Indian boyfriend. I hear Sylvia is in Kampala. I want the boys to meet her and then she can come back to the mine with me when the boys leave.

Lots of love,   Daddy

Haarkon's and Braaken's letter

I thanked Daddy for the lemon advice. I let Daddy know that President Kenyatta's visit was a huge event.

Throngs of villagers lined up along the seven miles in the steaming sun to the school cheering, *"Harambe,"* Kenyatta's motto meaning *pull together*. Policemen contained people at the roadside. The school, as well, was guarded. Being the school's art teacher, I was sure Sister Anastasia would introduce me to this great man when he visited the art exhibition hall. Nothing. Sister Anastasia had specifically said teachers will not meet the President but rather sit with our class directly in front of the visitor's stand, the hot sun upon us.

When the nuns brought in the mail I was anxious for my birthday card but disappointingly there was nothing for me. I couldn't believe I was twenty three. Time flies. I was glad Daddy had a nice time with his sons. Sylvia and Berit could have spent more time with them at the mine but Ulfhild would never allow that. I wondered if his ex-Australia wife, Marjory, would have invited us to the mine for holidays. White men in Australia had plenty half-caste children with Aborigine women. Many of those babies were forcefully taken from the *wild* mothers and brought in missionary schools; some were horrendously treated.

After Ulfhild left with the boys only then did Sylvia spend the rest of her holidays with Daddy.

> *Nyamolilo Mines Limited,*
> *Kabale,*
> *25ᵗʰ August 1968*

My dear Daughter,

Thanks for your letter of 8/8/68. I have just returned from Kampala where I have been very sick in hospital for a week soon after Ulfhild and the boys left for Norway on the 14ᵗʰAugust. Ulfhild was sick even as she entered the plane. I am not feeling well as the doctors told me I have a damaged heart. They advised

173

me to completely retire from work. How can I when everyone depends on me? I still have to maintain my Australian son whom I have never seen, Ulfhild and even my niece.

All this money can only be got by me working and just what I am not supposed to do. It's really not fair to be the only bread winner of strong, young, healthy people. I am starting to get very disillusioned about some of my children.

Berit has picked a child from God knows where with no parents, but this action, although is noble, is in fact very egoistical. She does not even have enough to provide for him. I hope she does not expect her ailing father to help.

I am alone on the mine now and find the work harder than ever. I am trying to find someone to buy the place and retire, but it is not easy.

I am not sure when I'll be back at the mine but when I do I shall send you some pocket money. I was sorry you did not meet your brothers. They too missed meeting you. They found Sylvia and Berit very pretty and questioned why you never met earlier but such was life then.

> *With lots love,*
> *Daddy*

I was shocked to hear Daddy was ill and in hospital. Just five years ago we had so much fun. I was so grateful that my sisters and I were on our way to supporting ourselves. I was unaware Berit adopted a boy. Later in life, she devoted many years working at an orphanage of many children who lost their parents through AIDS. She rode buses, Border-Border scooters and once fell off hurting herself. Among the four of us

174

Berit has done amazing good for children. A friend of mine had told me education was free in the Scandinavian countries. I gathered that should help with Daddy's sons. Helene was married. Daddy could no longer weather his hard and grudging existence. There was no way I could help him.

Nyamolilo Mines Limited
Kabale, Uganda,
3rd October 1968.

My dear Daughter,

Many thanks for your encouraging letter. I feel a bit worried because of your high blood pressure. It may not signify any serious disease; it may need only to be corrected which can be done these days with medicine.

The trouble with me, is that I have neglected or rather been ignorant of the fact that I had high blood pressure over twenty-five years and as a consequence my heart had to strain itself and got very large. This could have been avoided, if I took digitalis and diuretic had I known on time. You see, otherwise I am very healthy.

I want you to take an ELECTRO –CARDIOGRAPH and X-RAYS in order to find out if any damage has been done to your heart.

Now I shall advise you on banking your salary. I am doing this to you because you have always tried your best to get a move in this cruel world. I shall send Sylvia two thousand shillings -half is for you because I know what it is to be without a shilling. And in case I suddenly disappear, I'd like to know you have something to fall back upon. You have not been stupid to throw your life to some boy. Don't think I am against you girls marrying. I am not. But if you do find

175

someone who will treat you good and respect you and is intelligent and responsible then go for it.

Has Sylvia got a bank account like you? I'd like her to start saving as well. I saw Berit; she is young and foolish but will improve with years, I am sure. Berit said to me when I talked to her (where there is a will there is a way). What can I say? I am trying to advise all of you on your future as I will not always be there for you.

How big is your life policy? And with what company are you insuring? I do not trust an Indian company for instance, or a company that involves the government.

I had a visit from Mr. T. Demitrius yesterday and he wants to come back and work. I will take him and see how things go.

> *Lots of love my dear,*
> *Daddy*

What an experience I had with this guy coming over to the school and convincing me to open this policy. It seemed a good idea. In thirty years, when I'm over fifty I'll get 75,000 shillings. I'll not be cheated as it is an English company. I ran the whole story to Daddy.

The insurance salesman took me seven miles away at Thika for a checkup. I was a little uncomfortable as the doctor left the screen at the clinic opened and asked me to undress whilst the guy sat directly opposite me. After receiving the doctor signed forms a week later, I was to meet the salesman with a dinner at New Stanley with more forms to sign. Naïve me thought this is how new customers are treated. I wished Daddy was in Nairobi to advise me. I nervously asked Helene, who was visiting Nairobi, to accompany me at the New Stanley. When Helene met this very business-like man

176

she said *not to worry. He's an old man.* He had a bald shiny head like actor, Telly Savalas, in Kojak! Another part of opening the insurance was going to a movie and driven thirty five miles to school.

As we approached the school the car mysteriously stalled. He grabbed me and he tried to kiss me. I warned him if he as much as touch me, I'd get out of the car and walk to school. *Big deal!*

The sky was totally black without a star twinkling in the sky. Coffee plantations surrounded me with just a mud path enough for a car. Not a soul was around. Behind us was the spooky cemetery where the dead nuns arose and danced. I had high heels on. After my threat and silent prayer to the Blessed Mother Mary; I was silently taken safely to school. My Maltese friend was about to call the police as I had instructed her if I were late. Never again did I ever see this evil man. My policy was sent by post.

I should have listened to Daddy about insurances changing hands. I lost every penny I had saved at this insurance as it matured thirty years later!

> *Nyamolilo Wolfram Mine*
> *Kabale, Uganda,*
> *20/8/68*

Dearest daughters,

I just got both your letters of 17/9/68. God bless this wonderful post office in this country. Your letter clearly says P.O BOX 50 Kabale, Uganda and it was sent to Kitale Kenya!! It's so obvious these people cannot read. Next time put Kigezi as well; I was very pleased with your determination to get on in this difficult world. Your letters, you seem so sensible and loving. Thank you dears. I am pleased that everything is working out for you. I saw your mother and Berit and

177

Helene. They are spring cleaning the house. About time. I gave them money to get cement, and paint for the roof.

Yes, poor Ulfhild is still ill in the mental clinic in Norway. She is not, unfortunately, as strong as you girls. But that murder case she dealt with at the mine shook her to the bone! Haakon and Braaken are fine.

Now Mandy, I've told you over and over again these insurance guys and companies are crooks. You are lucky he did not do the worse then killed you and left you at the coffee plantation. You girls have to be very careful. Wish I could meet this guy and kick him where it hurts most.

Thanks for good wishes and I wish you and Sylvia a Merry Christmas although Sylvia will spend it on duty.

Yours loving,
Dad

I thanked Daddy for his letter and endless encouragement. I told him I did not believe doctors can cure chronic pains. I trained my body to live with pain. From a young age, I talked to my brain saying next week, next month, next year, when I'm a woman **I will be better.** Comforting myself lessen my pains. As for the emotional pain, I told myself unimaginable lovely stories putting myself to sleep. I was always hopeful for a better tomorrow. I saw so much poverty of hundreds villagers walking to masses from huts far beyond with children full of yellow mucus on their nose and covered with much flies about them. I was better off than many suffering people.

I thanked Daddy for helping with the roof. Hopefully, I should be home or I may go to the coast with my friends. It will be truly hot this time of the year. Once Sylvia went to the coast and came back as dark as me. I later suspected that caused her skin cancer in 1981.

Nyamolilo Mines Limited,
Kabale,
24th October 1968

My dear daughter,

Many thanks for your encouraging letter. I feel a bit apprehended about your high blood pressure. You have to find out what is causing it! You are young and can correct it in time. I have never realized I was suffering from high blood pressure over many, many years. As a consequence my heart is far bigger than it should be. I like you to have a good checkup and please report back to me.

I want you to do an electro-cardiogram and an x-ray in order to find out if any damage has been done.

Now, I've asked you about you opening a banking account of which you say you have done and you don't want me to help you now that you have a job. But you both have been intelligent and have good personality and I like to see you get on in this cruel world. I know what it is to be without a penny and in case I suddenly disappear from this world, I like to know you have something to fall back upon.

If you find someone you love make sure he is intelligent and responsible and trustworthy and someone who will be nice to you. Not someone who will use you and wreck your life.

Lots of love dear and don't worry about me.

Daddy

Daddy was still hopeful his heart could be fixed. He made several trips to Norway How do you fix an

179

enlarged heart? Twice he randomly wrote, in case, *I should suddenly disappear from this cruel world.* At fifty three, he was careful about diet; he took daily walked up and down the mountain. Like many a man, seeing a doctor for regular checkups was one thing never on his agenda.

I put his letter towards the light to see what word he had scribbled out and wrote DISAPPEAR instead. I remember just a year ago we visited him in hospital and he said, *"Every organ in my body is in perfect condition except the main machine."*

> *Bjordal Wolfram Mines,*
> *Kabale,*
> *24th November 1968.*

My dear daughter,

Many thanks for your letter of 30th September 1968. I have just received it! It seemed to be on its way for nearly one month! How can this be? Anyway I am relieved that you are feeling better, after your trip to Mombasa with your Bohora, Hindu and Sikh friends. Take care of your heart, you are still young. As I told you I never knew I suffered from high blood pressure until now and found I have a damaged heart.

I have a hypertrophy on the left side of my heart due to pressure for many, many years. I saw your mother off at the station. A change will do her good. I gave her pocket money.

Ulfhild is in hospital in a mental hospital in Oslo, the capital of Norway. Haakon and Braaken are fine. I got news that my father has got cancer and is about to die.

We are all suffering in this world one way or the other, unfortunately. I am as well as expected. Neither better nor worse. I have no help at the office. Mr.

180

Youhanous as you know; knows no English and has no clue in typing or book keeping, I regret to say.

Hope you enjoy the stay of your Mother in Nairobi. Best wishes and regards to all of you.

Lots of love

Daddy

Daddy had a plate full of problems in his life; the news of Ulfhild in hospital in Oslo worried him. I told him not to worry as Scandinavian countries have the best hospitals in the world. His religious, hardworking father, Jakob was ill with cancer. Luckily, Daddy got to see him. His mother died around the time he had seven children 1956.

We had a lot of fun Daddy and me: dancing after dinner, simply talking; we had quizzes on general knowledge. We tested him on religion including Church history hoping to put him down but he amazingly knew everything including in the Muslim faith questions. I truly believe, there was nothing my Daddy didn't know about.

Nyamolilo Wolfram

Kabale, Uganda,

12th November 1968

My dear Daughter,

Thanks for your letter of 28th October 1968. You say your pressure was 140/ 90 or less? At your age it should be 120/80. But pressure is a puzzling thing even for doctors, as sometimes a person may have high blood pressure and be in good health.

The crunch of the matter it is not pathological, that means constant high blood pressure without medication will eventually enlarge your heart to an abnormal size. Is your heart enlarged?

181

You don't want to lie in hospital to have an investigation done; you say it's too expensive? Don't worry, just send me the bill. If something is found it can be rectify with modern medications.

I would like as well to see your life insurance policy, even if it's under an English name. There are lots of swindlers in this world.

Poor Sylvia, she must be tired with night duties at the hospital. I had been on night duties as a young man, working on a roaring diesel engine on a ship at sea, as a sailor. I know what that is like. Tell Sylvia to write to me when she feels better.

Tomorrow I am going to Kampala. I am sick with the flu, AGAIN and sleep badly, but no doubt it will pass over as everything does in this world.

Love you

Daddy

My heart beat was always a little weird since six years of age. Doctor Smith discovered it but he didn't even put me on medication to regulate it. Instead he asked me why I had high blood pressure. *"Skinny and active people don't suffer from high blood pressure,"* Doctor Smith said. My dear Daddy was so concerned I might have the same problem as he. I told him I was fine. In fact, I recommended vitamin C for his colds, like he did not know that already. He had an orchard of lemon in the Impenetrable Forest of Uganda!

Sylvia was much better and doing as well as can be at Kenyatta Hospital. Sometimes, we managed to go dancing at a club called Small World. We did the jive, rock-n-roll, cha-cha, and the madison; nothing like Daddy's slow dances.

My Daddy's Great Grandkids

My Children and Grandchildren 2003

183

CHAPTER NINE
HE FINALLY SURRENDERS

Nyamolilo Mines Limited,
Kabale, Uganda
4th January 1969

My dear Daughter,

So surprised to hear you are married. I've just received your Christmas greeting card late as this marvelous post office sent it again to Kitale (Kenya). Aren't they so wonderful, and you clearly wrote Kabale. Well I am glad and congratulations. You've always been wise I noticed. Your husband's name is Louis surely that is not Italian but Seychellois. I take it; he took his mother's name. You are a woman now; I trust you will leave the nuns in a friendly manner. It helps. I am glad you found; what I hope, is a good man, but do not think that marriage is a sanctuary free from world's troubles. Fortunately, you are mentally strong. A good thing I know you won't feel so lonely anymore and you will have mutual understanding in love and sex if you are lucky. I've always had trouble with my married life. My wives, one by one, left me for one excuse or another. Your mother wanted to be with her family, Marjory wanted civilization in Australia, Ulfhild who stuck with me the longest time, was ever ill with depression, arthritis and mental illness. I'm not even blessed with seeing my children as often as I want to, except on rare occasions. Well my dear, this is my bad fortune but I have accepted it.

I still want to know your heart conditions, please.

How did your heart examination at the hospital go? You must send me the report on it please!

I had a houseful for Christmas, thirteen people in all sleeping here. My niece Berit is a fantastic person for organizing things. I'm completely worn out due to asthma, flu and bronchitis.

I got a Christmas card from Sylvia. She sounds lonely. Has she got a boyfriend? She is working on Christmas Day.

Well, my dear, send me a photo of both of you sometime.

Love to you and Romeo,

Daddy flew to Europe once again. Rumours said people with heart condition shouldn't fly. President Jomo Kenyatta, a man Daddy most admired and wanted me to meet, never flew because of his heart condition.

Daddy never used the train either. For transport conveniences, he'd rather drive himself. I had hoped he'd drive for my wedding to give me away but unfortunately, he was out of the country.

Because of the education he gave me, I vowed never to stop working even if it kills me.

Nyamolilo Mines Limited,
Kabale, Uganda,
14th February 1969

My dear Daughter,

Very many thanks for your letter enclosing photos of the wedding. I am awfully pleased that you are happy. Let's pray it lasts. You realize that it will not always be like that, but if you stick together in bad and good situations; you will grow fonder of each other. I

185

advise you not to have children at least in the first year. You know now there are so much pills and stuff these days so it is an easy matter to solve. I know being a Catholic it's against the Church's law but it's up to you.

Does your husband drink? As you know my bad experience with Seychellois who worked for me, ever drinking then becoming irresponsible. Seychellois are womanizers, as well. Anyway, without any reasonable doubt, I am sure and I do not think you would be stupid enough to mess your life. I have faith in you, Mandy, and believe your husband to be an exception. I also think it's wise to continue working for the time being before being a mother. Tell me a little about him; how you met? How long have you known him?

Please give him my best wishes. Maybe one day you both will come here on leave.

With lots of love,
Dad

I told Daddy the whole purpose of marriage was the joy of having a baby. Moreover, we Catholics do not practice birth control. The fifth commandment says *Thou shalt not kill.* I reminded Daddy that he gave me written permission and pocket money for my visit with Romeo's sister. We were sixteen and had a sisterly brotherly relationship that year of 1961. We met again almost seven years later when I visited Mombasa in 1967 at almost twenty-two years old. I had promised Daddy not to marry till I was twenty-four that I did not want children after thirty. That was too old! I promise never to give up working; the very reason he educated me through college. I remember what he once said, *"You educate a man you educate a person, you educate a woman you educate a family."* My children will do

186

well in school and go to University; I promised him. If I am lucky to see my grandchildren, I will teach them to read the easy way. Teaching is fun. I was glad I did not become an airhostess. I don't know if I'll pursue Daddy's dream and become a writer or an artist or a musician. I will at least fulfill one of them in time. But I was already pregnant.

Nyamolilo Wolfram Mine,
Kabale
29th April 1969

My dear Daughter,

Many thanks for your letter of 27/3/69. I am very glad you are happy with your husband and that you are both working harmoniously together. He sounds a reasonable character and apparently void of vices. About Sylvia, we missed our chance of seeing each other. I told her long ago as I had told you too, to give me ample warning as to when she expected to be in Kampala and this she disregarded. At that date, I had to rush and fetch my niece Berit who arrived from Mombasa. I had to rush back due to work. After arriving at Kabale, I got Sylvia's cable. I was so sad and disappointed as I missed my chance of seeing Sylvia this time, the opportunity just vanished. I received, as well a letter from the matron, that Sylvia had failed her examinations. That was another shock. You asked me about Helene. She does not write to me and neither does Berit.

My niece who was working at Mbarara is now working for me. The idea is she can look after the office work and I can go to Europe for a holiday and see my family as well. But the immigration has turned down her application for a visa. She says she will write to you soon.

I am not so bad these days although the high blood pressure was still up when I checked it in Kampala. It seems I have to take pills all the time to keep it down. We have been losing money on the mine for the last two months. It is not easy to make it pay all these new taxes these days.

With lots of love to you dear and regards to Romeo.

Dad

We already had that conversation about Romeo. We both worked and are slowly building ourselves up as he did. Daddy lived in a mud hut before a mansion. I believe he had us before he was ready for children; that's why he pointed out certain things to me like: *Have a savings before babies. No need to rush. With determination you will get there.* Drumming this into me and my sisters over the years it became annoying.

My baby, Helen, was baptized in Mombasa. What a great day that was. Romeo's sister arrived from England to be Godmother. Sylvia supported me with her presence. I would have invited my Daddy but he had left for Europe, yet again.

This was the first time I heard Daddy taking pills for blood pressure. I wished he had done that earlier on.

Bjordal Wolfram Mines,
Kabale, Uganda,
4th June 1969

My dear Daughter,

My congratulations to you both. Why didn't you tell me earlier about the coming baby? I was surprised that my Mandy had given birth! Thanks for your birthday card. Today is my fifty-fourth birthday. Just a word to tell you I am leaving on the 18th June. I shall probably be away for three months. My wife is still in hospital in Norway. In fact, she has been there for a year, so I have

188

*to go and see what is wrong with her. Looking through
some files the other day, I came across receipts I got for
your birth certificates and I hereby send them to you. If
you produce these to the office (Labone Office opposite
Dr. Aliker) you will be able to get them at once.*

*I wish that all goes well with you during my absence
and hope life will treat you well. I am in a flat-spin at
the moment having to fix so many things before I go.
Please send me a photo.*

With lots of love,

Daddy

Twice Daddy wrote to me on his birthday unaware
of it, I bet. With so many things happening in my life, I
forgot to tell him I was to have a baby. In those days,
one normally kept it to oneself until the baby was truly
born. Mishaps could happen. I could have an asthma
attack whilst giving birth and me or my baby die.
Despite throwing up, being very dehydrated and my
pulse dropping alarmingly low; I did pretty well. I gave
birth to a twenty-three inch tall baby girl after three
days of agonizing labour. Had I told Daddy, he'd have
been concern. In every letter Daddy, informed me how
ill Ulfhild was. At this time she was about forty-four.

Grand Hotel,

Kampala.

19th June 1969.

My dear Daughter,

*I am just writing a quick letter to say that I have
forwarded two thousand shillings to Sylvia and half is
for you.*

*I am sorry if I was mean in my last letter. I did not
mean to curse you. I had just had such bad news that
day and amongst other things the National Grindley*

Bank refused to give me more credit, but I've got that fixed now.

Tomorrow, I am living for Europe and I have had a hell of a time getting things fixed before I go.

Berit, my niece, has taken over the administrative work and Demitrius the technical. I hope and pray all will go well. Tell Sylvia I appreciate the card for my birthday and also thanks to you for yours. I hope you both do well. I am sorry for your certificates. I can see it's not your fault. Give my best regards to Sylvia. I shall send you some news when I arrive in Norway. Regards to Romeo.

Love,

Dad

I thanked Daddy for his letter of 19th June. My Daddy was actually apologizing for his letter to me of 1967! All was forgotten as far as I was concerned. However, his letter had shocked me. Daddy had never ever used a curse word on me. I had only wanted him to know how much I missed having a father my whole life. One thing I never blamed him. He was still right there in my *heaven,* where I left him. Daddy did not leave Mummy; she did. Even if he cursed me, that was fine. I understood he was an ill man. I should never have complained. Luckily, I have Romeo and baby Helen. Romeo seems loving, caring and hardworking just as Daddy was. That is what attracted me to him in the first place. To get peace of mind, I wrote to Daddy's niece asking for his address. She wrote back that she was not given instructions to give out personal information. This was my cousin! When she first met me she said, *"When Harald told us of having children with an African I thought you'd be half black one side and half white one side."* That was hilarious. I thought

190

of going to the Norwegian Embassy in Nairobi for help. Sylvia used to attend the Norwegian Independence day 14th May in Kenya every year

I missed Daddy terribly and I couldn't wait to introduce my new family. My adorable baby had the same blonde hair like her Grandpa. Everyone in Nairobi found it odd for two brown people to have a white baby with blonde hair. No one believed I too was once blonde; except my old school mates. Once an English workmate pointed out that my husband had jet black hair. *"Your baby looks nothing like her father!"* I asked her if she looked at the features or only at the skin colour and blonde curls. That shut her up.

Nedstrandsgaten
Haugesund, Norway
16/9/69

Dear Daughter,

I had a letter from Berit at the mine saying you wanted to write to me, but you didn't have my address. I am sorry, you can use the above. I have been thinking of returning soon as autumn is on in Norway and it is starting to get cold. I had wonderful weather in August. It was your birthday I remembered but am sorry I didn't send you a card this time. Happy birthday, dear; better late than never.

It was really nice in August for a change. When I came in July, it was miserable with rain and cold. On my way here, I stopped in London and I was very sick. It was a nasty bronchitis I got in London. In August, I visited my immediate family in Bergen where I was born and stayed there a long time as I know a lot of people. Most of my relatives live in Bergen. The weather changed and became beautiful and warm, so I had a lovely time.

191

When I was there Queen Elizabeth II and her family enjoyed their holiday in Norway. You know the royal family has every European blood running through their veins. Ulfhild and the boys visited me whilst I was in Bergen for some time but after a while they longed to be back at Haugesund where they live. When I went back to Haugesund, I found Ulfhild very sick. However, I figured she must be suffering with a lung infection, so I got her a new antibiotic, arythmesin, and after that she recovered. As for the asthma, she will have it for the rest of her life. I could have fixed that with hypnosis as I did with you when you were a child but there never was a more stubborn woman like my wife so now she can have her asthma. I have done what I could. Did you get my postcards?

Lots of Love, Daddy

Postcard from Daddy 1969

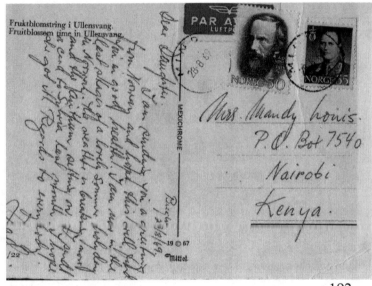

192

I was so excited Daddy sent me a postcard from Norway. He had a good rest and saw his family. I felt a little relief. I compared Daddy's two letters; one from Kampala and one from Norway, both written on the same day. Daddy thought of me. I made so much noise writing to the mine and was sorry about that. Daddy spoilt me by answering my letters immediately. I understood he was very ill on arrival to London. In Norway, he hoped to get good advice about his illness but instead he found Ulfhild ill. The *lousy* weather worsen his situation and he longed to be back in Uganda. I, too, hated Kenya's cold, depressing June to August weather. Those three months brought along colds and asthma. A letter from Norway cheered me up after feeling empty when Daddy left Africa.

Haugesund,
Norway.
6/10/69

My dear daughters Mandy and Sylvia,

Nice to have your letters and photo of you, Mandy and baby Helen. Berit forwarded your letters straight to me with request that I answer you immediately. She had no instructions from me to censure your letters. I should have given you my address before I left. I am glad you found a job in a European School. That is fine. But how do you manage with a child? She needs you much when she is young. Of course, you must be a caring mum. That also follows with time. What does Romeo say? That is what matters most.

You passed your exam, Sylvia. That is good for you. Yes, I understand you must have had a hell of a time but this will make you tough. You now need a good holiday.

I am annoyed at the bank for not sending you the money. When I come back I shall check and see if one

193

of the staff didn't put it in their dirty pockets (you know what I mean) About being alone, now that Mandy seems so happy and what have you, don't worry; you have plenty of time to choose the right man. Do not rush with marriage, it's a lifetime commitment. You are charming and very beautiful. It is a good idea to go abroad for further education. I will help you. But remember that it will be hard to enter into a new environment and meet strange people but it will be educational.

So you have new glasses. Never mind I am sure you look charming. Haakon and Braaken as well are wearing glasses.

I shall be leaving Norway on 11th October for London. From there I shall be leaving for Uganda on 16th October at eleven in the evening and arrive at Entebbe in the afternoon same day.

So my dear Daughters, I shall be back on the 16th October and I trust I shall be seeing you both sometime after this. So long.

Regards to everybody in Kampala.

With lots of love,

Daddy

I hoped my letter reaches him before he returned. I told Daddy how busy I was as a mother and teacher at a former English school. Majority of the staff are English and the Headmaster is called Mr. Mackintosh. I thanked Daddy for teaching me how to cope with reality.

R.E Hood, Barrister-at-law,
ADVOCATE
Notary Public and Commissioner of Oats,
Trade Mark & Patent Agent- Barclay Bank Chambers.
Kampala, Uganda
20/11/69

My dear Daughter,

Many thanks for your letter which Sylvia brought. No! It came by post long time after she arrived!! Can you believe it? Anyway I was so pleased to see Sylvia and I have thoroughly enjoyed her stay at the mine. She is a sweet and intelligent girl and I am very proud of her.

When I came from Norway I found such a mess and fired Berit; she must be on her way back to Norway. I, as well, 'learndt' to my horror other family affairs had gone wrong in my absence which Sylvia will give you an account. I was utterly disappointed that I could have died on the spot. Disappointments sicken me more than my heart ailments.

You, Romeo and little Helen are welcomed in April. Give me at least one month's notice as to when you shall arrive because of this lousy postal service.
Have a good time over Christmas and best regards to Romeo and Helene.

Love,
Dad

Romeo, baby Helen, and I picked Sylvia up from the station and she spent the night. I was all anxious to hear about my Daddy. She said he was as fit as a fiddle and they really enjoyed themselves.

Daddy, please drive safely back to the mine and take care of yourself till we meet in April. You must meet your granddaughter and my husband. I immediately replied next day 28th November not knowing Daddy was dead. We had kept in touch right up to the 20th of that November, just eight days before his untimely death. Although, I was happily married; cheered by my ever smiling toothless baby; I wished my family had spent a week or two with my Daddy.

195

Something within me had nagged me to visit Daddy. I cursed myself for not listening to my intuition.

Daddy looked great in the photo with a warm smile and a slight hint of the gold tooth on one of his incisors. Sylvia then showed me another photograph she took before they left for Kampala. Daddy looked aged; his flat stomach slightly protruding. *"Daddy doesn't look well at all. He never had a pouch."* I commented. Sylvia assured me he was fine but was upset about everything generally.

On twenty-sixth of November, Daddy picked Sylvia by the main roadside of our home and took her to the station. How they both cried when the last announcement to board the train was heard. Daddy watched the train snaking away, both still waving. Sylvia was so lucky to have Daddy drop her at the station something I always wished for when I was little as I watched other parents hugging and waving at their children. Tearful Mummy always saw us off for tens of years, I have no complains about her. I wondered if Daddy dropped his sons at the station. Normally white children travelled in different coaches on the same train. There were two departure days for schools. The nuns informed Daddy of our arrivals and departures beforehand.

Reading Daddy's letter made me feel like flying home and be with him for a while.

What did Daddy do after Sylvia left? We learnt from his doctor that on the 28th November Daddy had his check up for assurance to travel. *"Your father was fine,"* he told us. The Doctor seemed shocked. He did not believe Daddy dead. I must say the four of us were very brave, only confused not knowing what was going on. We thought that perhaps Ulfhild and their sons

196

would come and arrange the funeral. Perhaps, we would tag along on our own. We made inquiry at the hospital and were told the cremation was at the Hindu Crematoria at two in the afternoon. We viewed Daddy's body on the 2nd of December; he looked himself except for the sunburns and peeled skin at the upper cheeks. Sylvia, our nurse, said he did not turn blue as most white corpses she dealt with at Nairobi Hospital did. We said the prayer, *"May the souls of the faithful departed in the mercy of God rest in peace."* Daddy once wrote to me and said, *"We look to you as a strong brave member of the family"* I had to be strong. Moreover, I am a mother. Mothers are not weaklings. Again, Daddy had said, *"Ulfhild is not as strong as you, girls."*

We dressed formally in black. Mother babysat our four babies. We arrived at two-fifteen expecting to find Ulfhild and sons from Norway; his son R. David from Australia; government friends; Greek miner colleagues; missionaries he helped; a Grand Hotel representative, Louis Leakey's sons; and his body swathed in white upon a pyre. Perhaps, we shall see and hear a shaven headed Brahim priest from a Hindi temple clad in white loin cloth chanting the *mantra* and ringing a brass bell. Would we have the guts to watch ghee poured over the remains before the fire was ignited? Not a soul was there except the Norwegian Ambassador. I guess no one knew. God only let us know even though we were in Kenya and Helene was in Soroti.

Tens of years later, I attended the cremation of a Danish man, a friend of the Browns. I had sat by his bedside as he was dying at Nairobi hospital. He was made as comfortable as possible as he breathed his last

197

breathe. Nurse Gillian Brown found me there and said, *"Dying is difficult and painful."*

This man's cremation was done with dignity. His remains were smartly dressed and in a coffin. Hundreds of people, including me, silently stood as the cremation took place in an enclosed building. That is what should have been done for *my* Daddy. Had I found a melted gold tooth in the ashes I probably would have believed it was *my* Daddy's body.

Sitting on the verandah with Daddy admiring nature, as usual, he randomly said to me, *"Mandy, when I die and I'm cremated I want my ashes strewn over the mountain and my garden."* I did not like that hurtful comment even though I knew how passionately he loved his world. I should have carried those ashes and driven three hundred and fifty mile up to Nyamolilo and strewn them on his mountain and fulfilled his wish.

I enquired about my last letter to Daddy; begging Ulfhild for a few photographs of Daddy but was sent only those that I had sent him over the years. Now at sixty-five, for the first time, I have found the very photograph of baby Helen and me. At the back I had written, *"My dear Daddy. This your granddaughter Helen and I."*   *Love*

          Mandy

Filled with trepidations; I decided to go to town on the bus with baby Helen and Brother Richard. As we sat at a café having a cold drink and something for baby; I thought I was seeing an illusion. There was Ulfhild with a young man in a khaki outfit having coffee. He must have been a new lawyer. I went over and greeted her. Her face split up with a lovely smile. "Oh hello," she said quickly introducing me to the young man, as Mandy making sure not to reveal I had any connections with her. She rushed him to leave. I did however say, "*I am sorry for the death of your husband.*" She said, "Oh *well, thank you.*" She never gave me any condolences for losing my father.

I then introduced my ever smiling friendly baby. "*Oh my, she looks like any Norwegian baby.*" Touching the soft curls. "*She has blonde hair and white skin. Harald was looking forward to your coming in April.*" I wanted to tell her, "*Blood is thicker than water.*" She said she didn't carry money on her but that we should walk with her to the International Hotel. She gave my baby a hundred shillings to buy a present.

BJORDAL MINES LIMITED.
DIRECTORS:
H. BJORDAL
U.BJORDAL
18th March 1970

Dear Mandy,

I enclose some photographs that I found on the mine that probably are of interest to you and family. Perhaps you will pass them on to your sisters.

Demitrius wrote and said he had forwarded me a letter that had arrived from you to your father, but to date nothing has arrived. I presume there was nothing of importance. So far, I have only been able to raise shillings 16,000 that I had been asked to share amongst you. I am trying to sell the mine, but it will take time. Immediately I manage to raise more cash I will pay you.

Hope you and family are alright.

Ulfhild

"Daddy had told me "Demitrius cannot read or write!"

199

I was very upset Daddy's last letter vanished into thin air. When the world came tumbling down on him the month of November, I was unable to be with him. From the goodness of my heart I kept in touch with Ulfhild, at Christmas time, for twelve years after my Daddy's death. She too sent me a yearly Christmas card.

When Sylvia died in nineteen eighty-one I wanted Haakon and Braaken to know their sister had died. After all they had met in 1968; instead, a rude letter arrived from Ulfhild shocking me. *"I do not want you to have any connections with me or my sons. **Ever**! My sons suffered from traumas their life through!"*

In 1981 they were past mid-twenties. They were adults. Well, that was the last time I ever kept in touch with Daddy's family. *My sisters and I are hard core!* With God's guidance I found a couple of Daddy's photographs, his letters in a large envelope about to be discarded after Sylvia's death. I still regret not meeting my brothers in 1968. I've held to their little letters to date. Braaken surprisingly called me sister. Daddy laughed as he showed me the very first WILL he made without his signature. (*I did it when I did not have money. I shall now change it and leave everything to my children as no woman wants to stay with me.*) That was the unsigned paper that we received. I, too, laughed remembering what Daddy had said. *I had no money then.* What I have treasured most over the years were Daddy's letters and I am thankful he educated me. Every letter assured me of his love and concern on my future. Because Daddy praised America so much, here I am in Colorado, Daddy.

American Citizen Mandy Bjordal

Celebrating with Grandkids on June 20, 2012

CONCLUSION

What happened to your daughters, Daddy? Well, we have kept in touch forty-four years since your death.

Helene and George and their six children survived Obote and Idi Amin's politics and finally migrated to England. Sylvia married at thirty, had a baby daughter only to die of cancer when Lucy was just three years old.

Berit, the one who told you, *where there a will there is a way,* well she pursued her teaching career with determination and owns a school in Kampala. You doubted her adopting a child at eighteen; she worked at an orphanage mothering children who lost their parents through HIV. Berit has three children - two daughters, a son and several grandchildren.

I am now a retired grandma of six grandchildren living in beautiful Colorado, USA with my daughter Helen and two grandsons. Helen wanted to name her second son, Nicholas Harald but Bjordal was agreed upon. My second, daughter Jacqueline has two sons and lives in Canada. My son, Harald, named after you, has two daughters and lives in Canada as well. You have a part Australian grandson, Rennie from your son R. David. I have no idea where they are. I tearfully see you reincarnated in Haakon and Braaken on Facebook.

I almost jumped out of my skin when I found the Bjordal Mine still existed and your name is on the map, Daddy. The article explained Tungsten is found in quartz vein and still is plentiful but transport is inaccessible due to clayey soil. Unlike you, they could not manage with the floating bridge you had made and were thinking of having a helicopter fly over to carry tons of Wolfram, bismuth and other minerals. Your mine counted up to 30% of Uganda's export earnings. I asked about your home and was told not a stone is left upon a stone, no monument, not a reminiscent of my *heaven* remains. Just as you lost tons of Wolfram through theft, same thing happened to Krone and Bjordal Mine in 2004 and the mine closed down.

I've often dreamt of you, Daddy over the years. You never speak to me.

Recently, here in Colorado, I dreamt you came downhill to Namirembe, when I visited home. You waited by the roadside. Seeing you alive, I angrily rushed to the car crying and shouting at you, "How could you do this to me all these years; cheating me with your death?"

"Mandy, I was fed up with life generally. I now live in the depths of the Impenetrable Forest of Uganda. Well, I've come to take you live with me," he said firmly and I woke up with a start.

My last photo of my Daddy 1969

Rest in Peace Daddy and Sister Sylvia

IN MEMORIUM

MR. HARALD BJORDAL

IT WAS two years on November 28, 1971, since you departed from us. We shall never find another you the gap you left can never be replaced. You have gone forever but never will you be forgotten. We will remember you always and especially on that sad November day. Your wife and children.

HARALD BJORDAL
* 4. 6. 1913
† 28. 11. 1969

DEATH

SYLVIA Bjordal Hart died in London on 12/12/81.
Lord grant her peace.
Amen

IN
LOVING MEMORY OF
SYLVIA CHRISTINE HART
WHO PASSED AWAY
12TH DECEMBER 1981
AGED 34 YEARS

Bjordal Mine Reference Material

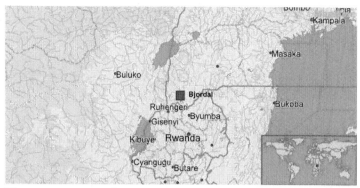

Tungsten occurs in quartz veins closely associated with granitoid intrusions at Nyamuliro (also called Bjordal Mine).

Tungsten (Wolfram)

Tungsten is used in the manufacture of alloys, armour plates, electric filaments and high-speed tools. There are at least seven small scale wolfram mines in Kabale and Kisoro districts and a small one in Buyaga Rakai District but those with the best potential to produce large tonnage are Bjordal and Kirwa mines. Bjordal mine was opened in 1947 and produced 2,000 tonnes of concentrates by 1983 when it closed. The mine has an estimated reserve of 10 million tonnes with an average grade of 0.5% WO_3.

http://www.comesatradehub.com/papers/mining.htm

The **Nyamuliro mine** is a large open pit mine located in the eastern part of Uganda in Eastern Region. Nyamuliro represents one of the largest tungsten reserves in Uganda having estimated reserves of 10 million tons of ore grading 0.5% tungsten. http://en.wikipedia.org/wiki/Nyamuliro_min

Nyamuliro Mine in Kabale district. The company was forced to shut down in late 2004 because of theft from the **mine. It is located on Plot ML4478 RUBANDA WEST in Kabale District of South Western Uganda** - about 435 Kilometers South West of Uganda's Capital-Kampala towards the Uganda-Rwanda-Democratic Republic Congo (Tri-National Border Corner). The Location of Krone (U) Ltd Wolfram (tungsten) Wolfram in Nyamuliro Wolfram Hills in Kabale has failed to exploit it. This is because of inaccessibility to the mine. There is a long stretch of swamp between Kabale and the mine, which makes it hard to transport equipment. Until the road is built and a bridge set up, the company will not be able to mine.
http://www.mining1.com/supplier/kroneuganda.html

Haugesund, Norway

Daddy's Final Resting Place- Our Saviour Cemetery

Made in the USA
Columbia, SC
07 October 2022